THE GOURMET'S GUIDE TO

COOKING WITH

BEER

First published in the United States of America by
Quarry Books, a member of
Quayside Publishing Group
100 Cummings Center
Suite 406-L
Beverly, Massachusetts 01915-6101
Telephone: (978) 282-9590
Fax: (978) 283-2742
www.quarrybooks.com

Library of Congress Cataloging-in-Publication Data
Boteler, Alison.
  The gourmet's guide to cooking with beer : how to use beer to take simple recipes from ordinary to extraordinary / Alison Boteler.
      p. cm.
  Includes index.
  ISBN-13: 978-1-59253-486-9
  ISBN-10: 1-59253-486-4
  1. Cookery (Beer) I. Title.
  TX726.3.B68 2009
  641.6'23--dc22

2008030925
CIP

ISBN-13: 978-1-59253-486-9
ISBN-10: 1-59253-486-4

10 9 8 7 6 5 4 3 2 1

Page layout: Claire MacMaster, barefoot art graphic design
Photography: Glenn Scott Photography
Food Styling: Catrine Kelty

Printed in China

THE GOURMET'S GUIDE TO
COOKING WITH

BEER

How to Use Beer to Take Simple Recipes
from Ordinary to Extraordinary

QUARRY BOOKS

ALISON BOTELER

Contents

intro All Hail the Mighty Beer 6

1 Appetizers 18

3 Pasta and Pizza 62

5 Poultry 108

Beerbecue 156

Sides 172

10 Breads 202

Soups
and Salads 2

34

Meats

78

Seafood 6

136

9

Brunch

186

11 Desserts

218

etc. Index 251
Acknowledgments 256
About the Author 256

Introduction

"In heaven there is no beer, that's why we drink it here!" . . . Or so goes the old polka song. Beer has certainly come a long way in its long, many-storied evolution!

These days, beer is chic: brewpubs, microbreweries, and fine restaurants have elevated beer tastings to the status of wine tastings. Some might argue that beer is a more intuitive pairing for many foods. There are fewer "rules" to abide by when drinking beer than for wine. Ask any beer aficionado and he or she will tell you that a Newcastle Ale goes great with fish 'n' chips. An ice-cold Corona takes the heat out of a fiery chiles con queso dip, since beer usually complements spicy dishes better than wine does. It's not hard to understand that a Blue Moon wheat beer goes well with seafood or to decide that a sweet stout tastes great with chocolate cake.

What Is Beer?

At its simplest, beer is an alcoholic beverage made from grain or another starch, such as wheat. Most beers are made from four ingredients: malted barley, hops, yeast, and water. How these ingredients are combined defines the many diverse types of beer. Their unique character begins during the brewing process.

THE BREWING PROCESS

Beer is usually made from barley, but sometimes it may be comprised part or in total of wheat or other grains, including millet, maize, and cassava in Africa; sorghum in Asia; potato in Brazil; and agave in Mexico. When the grain is soaked in water, the enzymes break them down into sugars that are then fermented with yeast. The fermenting sugars produce the alcohol. The entire fermentation

All Hail the Mighty Beer

varies according to the process used. (See "Fermentation.") The brewing process can be broken down into five categories: mashing, sparging, boiling, fermentation, and packaging.

Mashing

In the mashing step, the starch source is soaked in water at controlled temperatures so enzymes in the starch break down into sugars that can be fermented. Most mashes are made from malted barley. The barley grains are allowed to sprout and are dried in a kiln to make the *malt*, the sprouted part that contains the enzymes. The longer the malted barley is cooked, the darker the beer.

Sparging

The mashing process creates sugary liquid call *wort*. In sparging, also called *lautering*, the brewer separates the wort from the mash using a strainerlike gadget called a *lauter tun*. The brewer may rinse the mash to wash off extra sugars for the wort. The mash is either discarded or the brewer might try to reuse it, but doing so would result in a weaker and weaker wort.

Boiling

When all the wort has been gathered, the brewer begins boiling it down in a process that concentrates the sugar and also sterilizes the wort. At this point, hops are added during the boiling stage. Hops balance the sweetness of the malt.

Fermentation

The resulting mixture is then combined with yeast, the familiar fungus that is also essential for making bread. Yeast is used to initiate fermentation. These little micro-organisms consist of single oval cells that reproduce by budding and are capable of converting sugar into alcohol and carbon dioxide. Depending on the type of beer being brewed, the brewer may add quick- or slow-fermenting yeast in a process that can take from a week to months. During fermentation, yeast multiplies five- to eightfold and generates heat. The temperature is allowed to rise until it reaches 68°F to 74°F (20°C to 23°C) for ale and 54°F to 63°F (12°C to 17°C) for lager. At that point the fermentation is cooled to 59°F (15°C) for ale and 39°F (4°C) for lager, considerably slowing the yeast action. The yeast is then removed and the "green" beer, which contains about 500,000 yeast cells per milliliter, is then transferred to a *conditioning* or *maturation vessel*. At this point, a secondary fermentation may take place. Traditionally, the primary stage of fermentation used to take seven days for ale and three weeks or more for lager. These times have been shortened to 2 to 4 days and 7 to 10 days, respectively, by modern practices and techniques that use more efficient fermentation vessels. As the fermentation proceeds, the yeast settles to the bottom, leaving a clear liquid that may be subjected to further fermentation or made ready for consumption.

Packaging

The fermented beer is packaged in cans, bottles, or kegs. It may be artificially carbonated or it may be packaged with a small amount of yeast and sugar still in it, to produce a natural carbonation. Home-brewed beer is naturally carbonated but most commercial beer is carbonated (with some exceptions).

BEER TRIVIA

Throughout history, beer—insomuch that it is a beverage derived from fermented grain—was invented independently by many cultures. The first known civilization to make beer were the Sumerians. It is mentioned in their epic *Gilgamesh*, dating from the third century BC. After the fall of the Sumerian civilization, the Babylonians picked up where they left off, bringing brewing technology to new heights. Excavated clay tablets show that the Babylonians brewed as many as twenty different kinds of beer.

HOME BREWING BEER

For centuries, home brewing (as with most hobbies and food production) was the norm, before the advent of commercial breweries. In the United States, it came to an end for the same reasons that commercial brewing was almost wiped out: Prohibition. After 1920, the 18th Amendment to the Constitution forbade the making of alcoholic liquids for "beverage purposes." The repeal of Prohibition in 1933 did not affect home brewing, as a clerical error did not include beer in the definition of beverages that could be produced noncommercially.

In 1978, Congress repealed federal restrictions on home brewing. A number of books quickly appeared, including *The Big Book of Home Brewing* by Dave Line and *The Complete Joy of Home Brewing* by Charlie Papazian.

The process of home brewing mirrors that of commercial production, with a few important differences. First, home-brewed beer is not pasteurized. The pasteurization process requires the beer to be cooked, which kills the yeast and destroys the natural carbonation. Home brews, by contrast, contain live yeast and continue to undergo changes as they age "naturally." Commercial brews have to have the carbonation added after they have been pasteurized.

Another important difference in home brewing is that it often involves kits, which may contain malt extract. This concentrate can be added to water and yeast to begin the fermentation process without having to boil the wort. Home brewers can also mash their own grain and go through the entire brewing process.

Finally, home brewing allows the brewer to play with the parameters of beer making in a way that commercial brewers would not, ratcheting up the level of hops, for example, way beyond anything commercially produced, or altering the alcohol content.

TYPES OF BEER

Beer types are distinguished by the species of yeast used in their fermentation. The two main types of beer correspond to the two main types of yeast: top fermenting (ale yeast) and bottom fermenting (lager yeast). Ale yeast (*Saccharomyces cerevisiae*) is fast acting and requires brewing at higher temperatures. It stays at the top of the fermenting beer and leaves behind more sugars. It also leaves behind many esters, which give these beers stronger flavors. Lager yeast (*Saccharomyces uvarum*) is slow acting, sinks to the bottom of the fermenting beer, and leaves behind few sugars, which creates a drier beer.

Ales

Ales are produced by top-fermenting yeast at a higher temperature and tend to be full bodied, higher in alcohol content (4.5 to 6 percent), and higher in barley malt content. Ales can be further subdivided into other categories: pale ale, brown ale, dark ale, and cream ale.

Pale ale was available in England as far back as the seventeenth century, when the process of using coke fuel (a by-product of coal) to dry malt was developed. They are strong ales that are high in alcohol content (7 to 12 percent). They were well suited to overseas trade because the high alcohol content acted as a preservative.

Indian pale ale (IPA) has a very strong flavor of hops. In their colonial heyday, the British brewed it for shipment to India—they needed a beer that would stay fresh on long sea voyages. Its strong hops flavor acted as a kind of preservative.

Brown ales are made from dark brown malt and are sweet to moderately bitter with a low to medium alcohol content (4.5 to 5.5 percent). They are made with dark or brown malt, which have been cooked longer and are darker. These darker malts add chocolate- or caramel-like flavors to their brews.

These ales originated from England as well. Traditionally, the English brown ales have two regional variations. The ales from the north and eastern part of the country were hoppier and had a higher alcohol content, and the ales from the south were sweeter with a lower alcohol content.

Dark ales include **stouts** and **porters**. These dark ales are characterized by a rich brown coloring with caramel overtones due to the deep roasted malt. The deciding factor on whether an ale becomes a porter or stout is strength. Stouts tend to have higher alcohol content, and they can either be sweet (and less bitter) or dry. Irish stouts have a more bitter flavor and are higher in alcohol content than the sweeter English stouts. Porters were first brewed in eighteenth-century England. Porter was first brewed in Ireland in

1776. Guinness introduced theirs in 1778, and continued to brew ale as well until 1799. Extra-strong porter was called stout porter and eventually became what is today called stout. Stouts often feature a strong roasted malt that has overtones of chocolate or coffee. Interestingly, porters are undergoing a revival due the microbrewery movement; one can now find mocha and hazelnut porters among the many fine craft beers on the market.

Cream ales are a blend of both top-fermented and bottom-fermented beers. As the name suggests, they tend to be sweet and light in the hops flavor. Some are nearly dessertlike and are delightful after dinner.

Lager

Lager beers originated in Bavaria in the nineteenth century. These beers were stored in cold cellars or caves, where they would undergo a slow fermentation resulting in pale, more carbonated brews that have a lower alcohol content (4.5 to 5.5 percent) and are mild tasting.

Lagers can be further divided into pilsners, American lagers, and bocks.

Pilsners were developed in the Czech Republic in the nineteenth century. They are named after the city of Pilsner, where they were first brewed in 1842. These beers are clear, crisp, and carbonated, and are sweet with a strong hops flavor.

American lagers are particularly common in the United States, Mexico, and Australia but have attained some degree of popularity throughout the world. This style is characterized by beers that are light in color, low-to-moderate in alcohol content (4.2 to 5 percent) and low in hops flavor.

Other Lager Styles

Several Asian countries produce a number of lager-type beers. Many of their breweries were also established in the nineteenth century. In China, Tsingtao beer is brewed mainly for export. Japan produces Sapporo, a Bavarian lager-style beer, and Kirin, a similar lager. Thailand brews Singha, a German-style, hoppy, light lager.

Beerlike beverages have a long history in Mexico. They evolved from a Mayan and Aztec beverage of fermented corn or maize, long before the European conquistadors arrived. Another popular ancient beverage is *pulque*, made from aguamiel, a honey-flavored liquid from agave sap. *Mezcal* is a distilled spirit made from agave, and it is the precursor of tequila. The influence of German immigrants in the mid-nineteenth century led to the brewing of modern-day Mexican favorites such as Corona, an internationally popular lager-style beer. Negra Modelo and Dos Equis Amber were modeled after darker, more malty lagers brought to Mexico from Greece, known as "Vienna style."

British settlers in Australia soon found that the continent's extreme temperature changes affected the brewing, distribution, and storage of British-style ale produced there. The introduction of refrigeration in the mid-nineteenth century accommodated lager production, as well as enabling beer to be served cold.

Bock originated in Einbeck, in northern Germany, in the fourteenth century. It comes in a variety of colors including gold, light amber, brown, and reddish brown, and its alcohol content is relatively high (6 to 12 percent). It is a full-bodied lager with strong tastes of hops and malt.

Besides Ales and Lagers . . .

A few other types of beer or brewed beverages are not easily sorted into the ale or lager categories: wheat beers, lambics, and flavored malt beverages.

WHEAT BEERS

Wheat beers are brewed with the addition of wheat to the mash. These beers are called *witbier* in Belgium and *Wiesbier* in Germany, the name meaning "white beer." The wheat lends a sweeter taste and creamier body. In one type of wheat beer, *hefeweizen*, the yeast is not filtered out, giving it an opaque appearance. Other unfiltered beers may be referred to as "whites" because of this process. Their average alcohol by volume (abv) range is 4 to 7 percent.

LAMBICS

Lambics are beers brewed using wild strains of yeast and malted wheat. These beers are characterized by their fruity, acidic taste. This fruity bouquet comes from both the fermentation process itself and the addition of fruit syrups. They are brewed by a method called *spontaneous fermentation*, using naturally occurring yeasts. The only difference in the brewing is the yeast. These beers are typically made with 70 percent malted barley and 30 percent wheat. The wort is left in open air to acquire the yeast. Apparently, after years of brewing, many of these breweries contain populations of yeast in the brewing environment, which are allowed to inoculate the wort. These beers tend to be ciderlike or sour tasting. Faro lambic has brown sugar added and fruit lambics have a number of fruit flavorings.

FLAVORED MALT BEVERAGES

These are malt-based beverages to which has been added natural or artificial flavors to give the flavor of cider, fruit-flavored colas, or wine. Flavored malt beverages are a relatively recent trend infiltrating the beer case at liquor stores and supermarkets. Many consider these concoctions to be closer to "alcopops" than beer.

Popular International Brands of Beer

Type of Beer	Popular International Brands
Cream Ales	Genesee Cream Ale Little Kings Cream Ale Wexford Irish Cream Ale
Wheat Beers	Blue Moon Hoegarden Belgian White Beer Leinkugels Honey Wheat Beer Redback
Bocks	Einbeck Aass Bock Michelob Amber Bock
Lagers (American style)	Budweiser Coors Molson Michelob Honey Lager
Lagers (General)	Heineken Amstel Fosters Red Stripe Kirin Singha

(continued)

Popular International Brands of Beer (continued)

Type of Beer	Popular International Brands
Pilsners	Beck's St. Pauli Girl Krombacher Veltin's
Stouts and Porters (Dark Ales)	Guinness Stout Guinness Extra Stout Imperial Stout Fuller's London Porter Samuel Adams Honey Porter Sierra Nevada Porter
Brown Ales	Newcastle Brown Ale Oud Bruin Double Maxim Pete's Wicked Mann's Brown Ale
Pale Ales	Bass Pale Ale Worthington White Shield Sierra Nevada Pale Ale Orval Smithwick's Irish Red Ale Fuller's India Pale Ale
Lambics	Lindemans Framboise, Pomme, Cassis, Kriek, Pêche, and Gueuze Cuvée René Boon Faro and Gueuze De Troch Chapeau Mirabelle, Banana, and Lemon Cantillon Organic Gueuze Boon Framboise
Flavored Malt Beverages	Smirnoff Ice Mike's Hard Lemonade and Hard Limeade Captain Morgan Parrot Bay Tropical Malt Beverages

Microbrewing

Of great interest to beer producers is the growth of microbreweries. These craft brewers are changing the variety of beer types available to the consumer. In 1970, there were only forty craft breweries in the U.S., whereas now there are nearly fifteen hundred. Recently, the growth in sales of microbreweries' offerings has been steadily increasing while many national brands' sales have been relatively flat.

As mentioned earlier, Prohibition devastated the brewing industry. In the aftermath of Prohibition, only a handful of large breweries remained in the United States. These breweries attempted to appeal to a broad audience of consumers (including women) with a style of beer that was not particularly strong or flavorful. This is the first appearance of the American lager style of brew, which left the beer industry uninspired for decades.

Microbrewing appeared in Great Britain in the 1970s. The original definition of a microbrewery was a brewery that produced less than fifteen thousand barrels a year. This definition evolved to include the idea that small-scale brewing could compete with the large commercial brewers with its quality and uniqueness (as opposed to high-volume output and low prices of the large producers).

This idea spread to the United States in the 1980s, filling the yawning gap in variety that had been created by Prohibition and the subsequent restructuring of the U.S. beer market. U.S. brewers, some of them home brewers, rediscovered rich, regional, and international traditions of brewing and sought to incorporate them into their domestic brews. Microbreweries became known for innovation and variety in the beer market. Often, these early microbreweries were attached to or affiliated with brew pubs, which served beer brewed on site.

Since microbreweries don't try to appeal to a huge, homogeneous, bland market, they can focus on a niche market, meeting the demands for consumers who like something special. Some well-known microbreweries include Dogfish Head, Victory Brewing Company, and Sierra Nevada Brewing Company.

Why a Beer Cookbook?

Beer offers creative culinary adventure for cooks and has several properties that make it well suited for many dishes. Throughout this book, beer is used as a flavor-enhancing liquid ingredient. When stocking your "beer bar," consider keeping a bottle or two from several different types of beer for use in cooking or baking. It can be stored it in the pantry (it does not need to be chilled) for use at any time.

Beer can be used to marinate meats.
Beer used as a marinade will break down proteins and tenderize meats. A variety of flavors can be achieved depending on the style of beer selected. For example, a hearty stout or brown ale adds a deep glaze to grilled steak. Light lagers and pale ales are suitable for grilling chicken and fish. Poultry and pork are enhanced by marinating in lambics.

Beer is a simple substitute for other liquids in sauces and stocks, poaching, and for braising meats and vegetables.
Beer can be used in place of wine or stocks in traditional recipes. For example, this book spins a coq au vin into a coq au "Coors," substituting a lager-style beer for red wine. The result is an entirely different dish, and that's the point. Like home brewing itself, cooking with beer is as individual as the cook. A light wheat beer with a sprig of dill and a slice of lemon may be all it takes to turn poached tilapia or tuna steak into a divine dish.

Beer's yeast acts as a leavening agent that enhances batters and dough, and it adds moisture to baked goods.
When baking with beer, though, one must be careful about using it in a 1:1 liquid substitution. Beer in itself is a leavening agent. Many beer bread recipes do not even require yeast. Therefore, the recipes in this book are specifically designed for incorporating beer into the ingredients. As good as it might sound, it could be tricky to pour some stout in a chocolate cake mix without being able to make necessary adjustments.

The following chart offers general guidelines for incorporating beer as an ingredient in cooking:

The Beer Pantry at a Glance

Beer	Culinary Uses
Lagers	All-purpose beers: lighter lagers for poultry and seafood, cheese; darker, malty lagers for beef and pork. Also good for baking.
Brown Ales	Make an excellent marinade for beef and pork as well as liquid ingredient for stews
Pale Ales	The hoppy taste makes these a good marinade for poultry and pork as well as a braising liquid
Cream Ales	Good for poultry, cheese, and dessert dishes.
Stouts and Porters	Use in marinades for steaks and chops; produces rich-tasting sauces and glazes. Excellent for baking and desserts.
Wheat Beers	These have a delicate flavor, slightly acidic; they lend themselves well to cooking poultry and seafood.
Lambics	Fruity and light, these complement poultry and pork dishes and are the basis for many interesting desserts.

Appetizers

Stout and Stilton Pâté

Pâté often refers to a rich cheese and butter spread. In this recipe, shallots and garlic are sautéed in butter and simmered in Guinness Stout. This makes a great first course if packed into individual ramekins.

1 stick (¼ pound, or 112 g) butter

2 shallots, finely chopped

2 cloves garlic, crushed

½ cup (120 ml) Guinness Stout

Zest of ½ lemon

8 ounces (120 g) Stilton cheese, crumbled

⅓ cup (20 g) finely chopped fresh parsley

Salt

Freshly ground black pepper

Crackers or apple wedges

In a nonstick skillet, sauté shallots and garlic in butter until moisture evaporates or "sweats" and shallots are soft. Remove from heat and allow to cool. Add Guinness and lemon zest and simmer for 5 minutes. Stir in Stilton cheese and parsley. Blend in food processor until smooth and creamy and add salt and pepper to taste. Divide among eight to ten individual ramekins and serve with crackers or apple wedges.

Prep = 15 minutes   **Cook** = 12 to 14 minutes   **Yield** = 8 to 10 servings

Baby Beer
Burger Bites

Baby hamburgers have become a popular bar
appetizer in recent years. My father used to add
beer to hamburger meat before putting on the grill,
then toss in bread crumbs to absorb some of the
liquid. Later, I discovered that crushed
pretzels were a more flavorful substitute
for the bread crumbs.

½ cup (120 ml) beer
2 tablespoons (20 g) minced onion
1 tablespoon (17 g) steak sauce
½ teaspoon salt
⅓ cup (33 g) crushed pretzels
2 pounds (905 g) lean ground beef
12 to 16 mini egg-dough buns
     Ketchup
12 to 16 slices bread-and-butter pickle

Combine beer, onion, steak sauce, salt, and crushed pretzels in a
medium bowl until moistened. Mix in ground beef and shape into
twelve to sixteen miniature hamburger patties. Cook in a skillet or
on a grill for 4 to 6 minutes on each side until thoroughly cooked.
Serve warm on buns, topped with ketchup and pickle slices.

Prep = 25 minutes   **Cook** = 8 to 10 minutes   **Yield** = 6 to 8 servings

Drunken Beer Dogs

My parents used to drive us out in the country
to a restaurant called Indian Creek Inn. While
waiting in the cocktail lounge for a table for what
seemed like an eternity, we ate spicy little hot dogs
out of a chafing dish, leaving little room
for the delicious dinner ahead.

1 pound (455 g) hot dogs
2 tablespoons (30 ml) olive oil
1 seeded and chopped green bell pepper
1 onion, finely chopped
1 clove garlic, minced
1 bottle (12 ounces, or 355 ml) lager or pilsner
1 cup (240 g) ketchup
½ cup (140 g) chili sauce
1 tablespoon (15 g) spicy brown mustard
1 tablespoon (15 ml) cider vinegar
3 tablespoons (60 g) molasses

Cut each hot dog into four sections. Sauté in a large nonstick skillet
in olive oil along with bell pepper, onion, and garlic until onions are
tender. Add beer, ketchup, chili sauce, mustard, vinegar, and
molasses. Simmer until liquid is reduced by half and the consistency
of thick barbecue sauce. Serve in a chafing dish as an appetizer.

Prep = 15 minutes   **Cook** = 35 to 40 minutes   **Yield** = 8 servings

Beer Cheese Spread

This classic beer cheese spread is great
when broiled, open faced, on thick slices of toast
for a grilled cheese sandwich. Or spread it on toasted
crostini and top it with some olives or chopped
tomato, and you'll have beer cheese bruschetta.

2 pounds (905 g) sharp Cheddar cheese, shredded
1 small onion, chopped
2 cloves garlic, crushed
½ teaspoon hot sauce
1 bottle (12 ounces, or 355 ml) amber beer (room temperature)
Salt and pepper
English muffins

Combine cheese, onion, garlic, and hot sauce in a food processor.
While motor is running, gradually pour in beer and blend until
creamy. Season with salt and pepper to taste.

Chill for at least 3 hours before serving. Of course, this can be
used as a cold spread or a dip, but it can also be broiled on top of
English muffins, toast, or crostini.

Prep = 15 minutes   **Chill** = 3 hours   **Yield** = 8 to 12 servings

Thai Chicken Wings with Peanut Sauce

Thailand's trademark beer, Singha, is a natural accompaniment for Thai chicken wings. Singha is a medium yellow beer that could be used interchangeably with any domestic brand you happen to have around the house.

  2 tablespoons (32 g) creamy peanut butter
  1 tablespoon (15 ml) lime juice
  2 teaspoons (10 ml) soy sauce
  2 teaspoons (4 g) grated fresh ginger
  ½ cup (130 g) salsa
  ¼ cup (60 ml) Singha or other beer
  2 dozen chicken drummettes (drumstick end of disjointed chicken wings)

PEANUT SAUCE:
  ½ cup (130 g) creamy peanut butter
  ½ cup (100 g) sugar
  3 tablespoons (45 ml) light soy sauce
  ½ cup (120 ml) Singha beer
  1 clove garlic, crushed
  ½ teaspoon red pepper flakes
  ½ teaspoon sesame oil

Preheat oven to 400°F (200°C, or gas mark 6). In a medium bowl, blend peanut butter with lime juice, soy sauce, and ginger until smooth. Stir in salsa and blend in beer. Toss drummettes in peanut butter mixture and arrange in a roasting pan or baking dish lined with foil. Bake wings for 20 to 30 minutes, until no longer pink inside and nicely glazed. Serve warm with peanut sauce.

For peanut sauce: Combine peanut butter, sugar, soy sauce, beer, garlic, red pepper flakes, and sesame oil in a small saucepan, stirring until mixture is smooth and heated through. Sauce will thicken as it stands.

Prep = 20 minutes   **Cook** = 30 minutes   **Yield** = 6 to 12 servings

Portobello Mushroom Caps with Porter-Caramelized Onions

Rich caramelized onions are well worth the patience required to turn raw slices into savory vegetable candy. Adding a dark beer such as a porter (an extra-dark stout) helps the onions take on a rich amber color and complex flavor.

3 tablespoons (42 g) butter

1 tablespoon (15 ml) olive oil

6 cups (690 g) thinly sliced Vidalia onions

1 teaspoon minced fresh thyme (optional)

¼ teaspoon salt

1 teaspoon sugar

4 to 5 tablespoons (60 to 75 ml) porter or extra-dark stout

½ cup (68 g) toasted pine nuts

8 portobello mushroom caps

Garlic oil-flavored nonstick cooking spray

Melt butter with olive oil in a large nonstick skillet. Add onions, thyme, salt, and sugar. Cook, stirring over medium heat, until onions begin to soften, about 5 minutes. Reduce heat to low and continue cooking and stirring onions until rich and golden brown, deglazing pan with beer as liquid starts to evaporate and onions start to brown in the bottom of the pan. The total process takes about 20 minutes and you may have to deglaze the pan two or three times, adding as much beer as necessary. Stir in pine nuts.

Meanwhile, preheat oven to 425°F (220°C, or gas mark 7). Line a baking sheet with aluminum foil and coat with nonstick spray. Place mushroom caps on foil with the top of the caps facing up and cover with another coat of spray. Bake for 5 to 8 minutes, until the mushrooms start to shrink. Remove from oven and turn stem side up. Fill mushroom caps with the onion mixture. Return to oven and bake for another 5 to 8 minutes.

Note: To toast pine nuts: Coat a nonstick skillet with a thin coating of olive oil and sauté pine nuts until they are a light golden brown.

Prep = 20 minutes   **Cook** = 35 to 40 minutes   **Yield** = 8 servings

Pepperoni Pizza and Beer Dip

This appetizer can be made ahead,
refrigerated, and placed under the broiler
at the last minute.

1½ packages (8 ounces, or 225 g, each) cream cheese, softened
2 cloves garlic, crushed
2 tablespoons (10 g) grated Parmesan cheese
½ cup (125 g) pizza sauce, divided
⅓ cup (80 ml) beer
½ cup (75 g) chopped pepperoni
1 can (2.25 ounces, or 62 g) ripe olives, drained
⅓ cup (50 g) seeded and finely diced red bell pepper
½ cup (50 g) sliced scallions
½ cup (60 g) shredded mozzarella cheese
Bread sticks or pita chips

Beat cream cheese with garlic and Parmesan cheese until soft.
Blend in ¼ cup (65 g) of pizza sauce and the beer. Spread on an
ovenproof serving platter. Top with pepperoni, olives, bell pepper,
and scallions. Drizzle with remaining pizza sauce and top with
cheese. Broil 4 inches (10 cm) from heat, or until mozzarella is
melted and bubbling. Serve hot with bread sticks or pita chips.

Prep = 10 minutes   **Cook** = 4 minutes   **Yield** = 12 servings

Buffalo Beer Wings

Everyone's bar favorite just gets better with
a little beer. It's simmered right into the sauce. You
can increase or decrease the amount of hot sauce
depending on your own taste preference.

2½ pounds (1.13 kg, about a dozen) chicken wings
⅓ cup (75 g) butter
4 cloves garlic, minced
1 shallot, minced (optional)
1 onion, finely minced (optional)
⅓ cup (80 ml) beer
⅓ cup (75 g) hot sauce, plus extra for dipping
Pinch of sea salt
Vegetable or peanut oil, for frying
Blue cheese dressing
Celery sticks

Split the wings at each joint and discard tips. Rinse and pat dry with
paper towels.

Meanwhile, in a small saucepan, melt butter over low heat, with
minced garlic. Add minced shallot and onion (if using), and sauté
until tender. Add beer, hot sauce, and sea salt, then simmer until
liquid is reduced by about half. Puree with a stick blender to smooth
out sauce, and keep hot.

Preheat oil in a deep fryer to 450°F (230°C). When the oil is the
correct temperature, carefully lower the wings into the hot oil, using
a slotted spoon or wire basket, and deep-fry for about 12 minutes, or
until wings are cooked and crispy. Drain on paper towels. Toss with
the hot beer sauce, coating several times to cover well. Serve with a
side of extra hot sauce for dipping, a bowl of blue cheese dressing,
and celery sticks.

Prep = 25 minutes   **Cook** = 25 minutes   **Yield** = 4 servings

Swiss-Style Beer Cheese Fondue

Traditional Swiss fondue is made with
white wine and a spike of kirsch. However,
some are made with beer, which gives them a whole
new character. Try an imported Swiss or German
beer for an authentic alpine effect.

8 ounces (225 g) Emmentaler cheese, grated
4 ounces (115 g) Gruyère cheese, grated
1 tablespoon (8 g) all-purpose flour
1 clove garlic, halved
¾ to 1 cup (175 to 235 ml) beer
French bread cubes
Crisp apple wedges

In a bowl, toss grated cheeses with flour until evenly coated. Rub
fondue pot with garlic clove. Add ¾ cup (175 ml) of beer and heat
slowly over low heat. Add cheese mixture by handfuls, stirring constantly until cheese is melted and smooth. If fondue becomes too
thick, it can be thinned down with additional beer.

Serve with skewers for dipping bread cubes and apples.

Prep = 10 minutes   **Cook** = 10 to 15 minutes
Yield = 10 to 12 servings

Lambic Hot Crab Dip

It just wouldn't be a party
without crab dip. Lambic beers are elegant
complements for most seafood.

 1 package (8 ounces, or 115 g) cream cheese, softened
⅓ cup (33 g) grated Parmesan cheese
⅓ cup (38 g) shredded Monterey Jack cheese
⅓ cup (156 ml) Blue Moon or other lambic beer
⅓ cup (75 g) mayonnaise
¼ cup (30 g) minced celery
¼ cup (25 g) finely sliced scallions (about 4)
½ teaspoon garlic powder
½ teaspoon Worcestershire sauce
 1 cup (200 g) cooked crabmeat, picked over for cartilage
½ cup (69 g) toasted almonds (see Note)

In a large bowl, with an electric mixer, beat the three cheeses together. Slowly beat in beer until blended. Mix in mayonnaise, celery, scallions, garlic powder, Worcestershire sauce, and crabmeat. Preheat oven to 375°F (190°C, or gas mark 5). Spread crab mixture in a 9-inch (23 cm) ungreased pie plate or shallow 1-quart (1 L) casserole dish. Bake for 15 to 20 minutes, or until hot and bubbly.

Note: To toast almonds: Preheat oven to 350°F (180°C, or gas mark 4) and spread almonds on a baking sheet. Bake for 6 to 8 minutes, stirring once or twice, until evenly golden brown. Watch carefully to avoid burning.

Prep = 20 minutes   **Cook** = 15 to 20 minutes
Yield = 12 servings

Chiles con Queso Reduction

This version of chiles con queso
is simmered with beer in a reduction of
onion, garlic, chiles, and tomatoes.

½ stick (4 tablespoons, or 55 g) butter
1 onion, finely chopped
1 clove garlic, crushed
1 can (4 ounces, or 115 g) mild green chiles, drained and chopped
1 can (15 ounces, or 425 g) diced tomatoes, drained
½ cup (120 ml) Corona beer
½ teaspoon salt
½ cup (120 ml) light cream
2 cups (230 g) shredded Monterey Jack cheese
⅓ cup (43 g) sliced ripe olives
Tortilla chips

Melt butter in a medium skillet. Sauté onion, garlic, chiles, and tomatoes until onions are soft. Add beer and simmer for 15 to 20 minutes over low heat, or until most of the liquid has evaporated. Add salt, cream, and cheese, and blend until smooth, similar to the consistency of thick gravy. Stir in olives.

Serve in a fondue pot or chafing dish, with tortilla chips for dipping.

Prep = 15 minutes   **Cook** = 20 to 25 minutes
Yield = 8 to 10 servings

Soups
and Salads

Porter Sweet Potato Salad

Sweet potato salad is simply a wonderful change of pace to serve at picnics with fried or grilled chicken. Simmer the potatoes in porter, which adds character to the dish.

1 pound (455 g) sweet potatoes or yams
1 bottle (12 ounces, or 355 ml) porter
1 ½ cups (353 g) mayonnaise
½ teaspoon salt
¼ teaspoon pepper
2 tablespoons (30 g) brown sugar
1 tablespoon (15 ml) cider vinegar
1 tablespoon (16 g) prepared mustard
1 cup (120 g) chopped celery
4 scallions, thinly sliced
1 can (16 ounces, or 455 g) pineapple chunks, very well drained
½ cup (40 g) crisp crumbled cooked bacon

Peel sweet potatoes and cut into 1-inch (2.5 cm) cubes. Place in a very large saucepan and add beer. Add enough water to cover potatoes. Bring to a boil and cook for 25 to 30 minutes, or until fork tender but not mushy. Drain in colander and let cool, then chill for at least 2 hours.

In a large bowl, combine mayonnaise, salt and pepper, brown sugar, vinegar, and mustard until smooth. Stir in celery and scallions. Cut pineapple chunks in half and stir in, along with bacon. Gently mix in potatoes last so as not to break them up too much. Chill for at least 2 hours longer before serving.

Prep = 25 minutes   **Cook** = 30 minutes
Chill = 4 hours   **Yield** = 8 servings

Wisconsin Beer and White Cheddar Wild Rice Soup

The medley of wild rice, white Cheddar, and beer is instantly comforting as well as delicious. This falls into that category of "feel-good" food.

⅔ cup (150 g) butter
½ cup (75 g) minced shallots
1 cup (120 g) shredded carrots
½ cup (60 g) chopped celery
3 tablespoons (28 g) seeded and minced green bell pepper
⅔ cup (75 g) all-purpose flour
1 teaspoon dry mustard
1 teaspoon salt
1 can (10¾ ounces, or 306 ml) chicken broth
3 cups (710 ml) milk
1 cup (235 ml) half-and-half
1 can (12 ounces, or 355 ml) beer
3 cups (338 g) shredded white Cheddar cheese
1½ cups (227 g) cooked wild rice

Melt butter over medium heat in a large saucepan and sauté shallots, carrots, celery, and green pepper until tender. Blend in flour, mustard, and salt. Blend in chicken broth, milk, half-and-half, and beer with a wire whisk. Cook, whisking constantly, until mixture comes to a boil and thickens. Blend in cheese until melted and stir in wild rice.

Prep = 25 minutes   **Cook** = 20 minutes   **Yield** = 6 servings

Asian Beer-Chicken Soup

This is a quick and simple soup
that really doesn't require hours of simmering
on the stove. The fortifying ginger helps
clear the head, especially during
winter cold and flu season.

3 cans (14 ounces, or 425 ml, each) chicken broth
1 can or bottle (12 ounces, or 355 ml) Asian beer,
   such as Tsingtao, Asahi, or Kirin
¾ cup (175 ml) water
1 tablespoon (8 g) grated fresh ginger
1 clove garlic
¼ teaspoon red pepper flakes
4 ounces (115 g) uncooked soba noodles or whole wheat spaghetti
½ cup (60 g) grated carrot
2 boneless, skinless chicken breasts, sliced very thin
1 medium red bell pepper, seeded and sliced into thin strips
1 cup (75 g) snow peas, sliced ½ inch (1.2 cm) long on the diagonal
   Juice of 1 lime
2 scallions, thinly sliced
   Salt and pepper

In a large saucepan, bring broth, beer, water, ginger, garlic, and red
pepper flakes to a boil. Add noodles and carrots, and lower heat to
a simmer. Cook until tender, about 8 minutes. Add chicken, bell
pepper, and snow peas. Cook until chicken is opaque throughout,
2 or 3 minutes. Add lime juice, scallions, and salt and pepper to taste.

Prep = 20 minutes   **Cook** = 20 minutes   **Yield** = 4 servings

Baby Bella Mushroom and Beer Soup

For this hearty soup,
the mushrooms simmer in beer
for hours in a slow cooker.

 1 pound (455 g) sliced baby bella mushrooms
 1 can (14 ounces, or 425 ml) chicken broth
 2 cans or bottles (12 ounces, or 355 ml, each) beer
 3 cloves garlic, crushed
12 scallions, rinsed and sliced
 2 red bell peppers, seeded and chopped
 3 tablespoons (45 g) sun-dried tomato paste
 1 teaspoon salt
 1 tablespoon (15 ml) Worcestershire sauce
 ½ stick (4 tablespoons, or 55 g) butter
 ¼ cup (31 g) all-purpose flour
 ½ cup (120 ml) light cream

In a slow cooker, combine mushrooms, chicken broth, beer, garlic, scallions, red bell peppers, sun-dried tomato paste, salt, and Worcestershire sauce. Cover and cook on low setting for 6 hours. In a medium saucepan over medium heat, melt butter and stir in flour, blending with a wire whisk until smooth and bubbling. Blend in light cream and cook, stirring constantly, until mixture thickens. Add some broth from the soup to the cream sauce and blend with a wire whisk, then add the cream sauce back to the soup, using the whisk to smooth out any lumps.

Prep = 15 minutes   **Cook** = 6 hours 10 minutes   **Yield** = 8 servings

Chicken Chili with Beer and Black Beans

This chili is lighter than most recipes,
and cornmeal helps thicken the beer broth.

½ cup (80 g) diced red onion
3 tablespoons (45 ml) olive oil
3 cloves garlic, crushed
1 red bell pepper, cored, seeded, and diced
1 jalapeño, seeded and diced
1 tablespoon plus 1 teaspoon (20 g) chili powder
2 teaspoons (5 g) ground cumin
2 teaspoons (1.5 g) dried basil
2 quarts (2 L) chicken broth
1 can (14.5 ounces, or 411 g) diced tomatoes, undrained
1 can (12 ounces, or 355 ml) plus 3 tablespoons (45 ml) dark beer
3 tablespoons (45 ml) Worcestershire sauce
¼ cup (35 g) cornmeal
¼ cup (5 g) chopped fresh cilantro
½ teaspoon salt
½ teaspoon pepper
4 cups (560 g) shredded cooked chicken
2 cups (500 g) canned black beans, drained and rinsed

In a large stockpot, sauté onion in olive oil over medium heat until soft, about 10 minutes. Add garlic and peppers, and sauté for 1 more minute. Add chili powder, cumin, and basil, and cook, stirring, for 2 to 3 minutes. Add broth, tomatoes, beer, and Worcestershire sauce. Increase heat and bring to a boil. Add cornmeal, cilantro, salt, pepper, chicken, and beans. Simmer for another 15 minutes.

Prep = 20 minute   **Cook** = 30 minutes   **Yield** = 6 to 8 servings

Danish Potato Soup with Beer

Danish lagers or pilsners are perfect for this hearty ham and potato soup, although pilsner or lagers of any provenance will work just as well.

2 bottles (12 ounces, or 355 ml, each) Danish or domestic lager or pilsner
1 can (14 ounces, or 425 ml) chicken broth
1 ham bone
2 potatoes, peeled and diced
8 scallions, sliced
4 celery stalks, chopped
¼ cup (15 g) minced fresh parsley
2 cups (180 g) chopped cabbage
2 carrots, diced
3 tablespoons (42 g) butter
3 tablespoons (24 g) all-purpose flour
1 cup (235 ml) light cream
Grated nutmeg

Combine beer, chicken broth, and enough water to measure 2 quarts (950 ml) in a soup kettle. Add ham bone and bring to a boil. Reduce heat and simmer for 1 hour, or until meat pulls away from the bone. Remove ham bone. When cool enough to handle, trim off any meat and dice. Discard bone. Return ham to kettle along with potatoes, scallions, celery, parsley, cabbage, and carrots; cook for 40 minutes.

In a small saucepan over medium heat, melt butter and blend in flour, cooking to make a bubbly paste or roux. Blend in cream and cook, blending constantly, until sauce thickens. Remove from heat. Blend about a cup of soup liquid into sauce and then blend sauce into soup kettle. Sprinkle a pinch of nutmeg on each bowlful just before serving.

Prep = 25 minutes   **Cook** = 1 hour 45 minutes   **Yield** = 6 servings

Fresh Tomato and Beer Soup

Anyone with a vegetable garden knows that by the end of summer, tomatoes are given away to everyone, including the postman. Here is a perfect recipe for a bumper crop.

6 cups (900 g) chopped fresh tomatoes
1 slice onion
4 whole cloves
1 can (12 ounces, or 355 ml) beer
2 cups (475 ml) chicken broth
3 tablespoons (45 g) butter
3 tablespoons (24 g) all-purpose flour
1 tablespoon (13 g) sugar
1 teaspoon salt, or to taste

In a stockpot, over medium heat, combine the tomatoes, onion, cloves, beer, and chicken broth. Bring to a boil, and gently boil for about 20 minutes to blend all of the flavors. Remove from heat and run the mixture through a food mill into a large bowl or pan. Discard whatever solids are left over in the food mill.

Rinse out stockpot and melt the butter over medium heat. Stir in the flour to make a bubbling paste or roux, cooking until the roux is a medium brown. Gradually whisk in a bit of the tomato mixture, so that no lumps form, then stir in the rest. Season with sugar and salt, and adjust seasonings to taste.

Prep = 15 minutes   **Cook** = 30 minutes   **Yield** = 6 to 8 servings

Stout Onion Soup Gratin

Combining stout with caramelized onions turns classic French onion soup into a new experience. Try using potato bread for the croutons.

POTATO BREAD CROUTONS:
- 3 cups (90 g) potato bread cubes
- 3 tablespoons (42 g) butter, melted
- 1 tablespoon (15 ml) olive oil
- ¼ cup (25 g) grated Parmesan cheese

SOUP:
- 2 tablespoons (30 ml) olive oil
- 2 tablespoons (28 g) butter
- 3 large yellow or Vidalia onions, sliced
- 6 cups (1425 ml) beef stock divided
- 2 bottles (12 ounces, or 355 ml, each) Guinness Extra Stout
  Salt and pepper
- 1 bay leaf
- 1 teaspoon dried thyme
- 1 cup (110 g) shredded Swiss cheese

For the potato bread croutons: Preheat oven to 375° F (190°C, or gas mark 5). Toss bread with butter, oil, and cheese. Spread in a 9 × 13-inch (22.5 × 32.5 cm) baking pan. Bake for 10 to 15 minutes, stirring twice, until golden brown and toasty (being careful not to burn).

For the soup: Heat olive oil and butter in a large nonstick stockpot. Add onions. Cook, stirring over medium heat, until onions begin to soften, about 5 minutes. Lower heat and continue cooking and stirring onions until rich and golden brown, deglazing pan with a little beef broth as liquid starts to evaporate and onions start to brown in the bottom of the pan. The total process takes about 20 minutes and you may have to deglaze the pan two or three times. Add remaining beef broth and beer, and a little salt and pepper to taste. Add bay leaves and thyme. Cover and simmer for 20 minutes. Divide soup among six to eight ovenproof crocks. Top with croutons and shredded cheese; broil until the cheese melts.

Prep = 20 minutes   **Cook** = 50 to 60 minutes
Yield = 6 to 8 servings

Oxtail, Lentil, and Lager Onion Soup

My grandmother used to make oxtail soup on the stove top but slow cookers have made the process so much easier. It's liberating not having to "watch the pot" and a perk of this recipe is the wonderful aroma wafting through the house for the full seven hours of cooking time.

2 teaspoons (10 ml) olive oil

1 pound (455 g) oxtail bones

1 ½ cups (195 g) chopped carrots

1 ½ cups (180 g) sliced celery

1 cup (192 g) uncooked lentils

2 teaspoons (2 g) dried thyme

1 bay leaf

⅛ teaspoon salt

¼ teaspoon black pepper

1 can or bottle (12 ounces, or 355 ml) lager

2 cups (475 ml) water

1 can (10½ ounces, or 299 ml) condensed onion soup

In a large nonstick skillet, brown oxtails on both sides in olive oil. Put carrots, celery, lentils, thyme, bay leaf, salt, and pepper in a slow cooker. Cover with oxtails. Pour beer, water, and onion soup over mixture. Cover and cook on low setting for 7 hours or on high setting for 3 ½ hours, or until meat and lentils are tender.

Remove oxtails from soup. Pull meat from bones and cut into small pieces. Return meat to soup and serve.

Prep = 15 minutes   **Cook** = 3 hours 40 minutes (on high setting) or 7 hours 10 minutes (on low setting)   **Yield** = 4 servings

Game Day Beer Cheese Soup

What is it about snack cheese, popcorn, pretzels, and beer that make the perfect combination to snack on while the match is on TV? This recipe uses pretzel nuggets or popcorn in place of croutons as a soup topper.

⅓ cup (75 g) butter
⅔ cup (110 g) chopped onion
⅓ cup (41 g) all-purpose flour
3 cups (710 ml) milk
⅔ cup (156 ml) flat beer
1 jar (15 ounces, or 427 g) Cheez Whiz
Salt and pepper
Fresh buttered popcorn or pretzel nuggets

Melt butter in a large saucepan over medium heat and sauté onions until tender. Blend in flour with a wire whisk until smooth and bubbling. Gradually whisk in milk and beer. Cook, stirring constantly, until bubbling, smooth, and thickened. Add Cheez Whiz and blend until heated through and smooth. Season with salt and pepper to taste. Serve in cups or bowls topped with popcorn or pretzels.

Prep = 5 minutes **Cook** = 10 minutes
Yield = 6 to 8 servings

Steak and Stout Stew

Save the ends of overdone London broil in the freezer, and eventually there will be enough for this soup, enhanced by the flame-grilled beef and a rich stock laced with stout.

    1 stick (¼ pound, or 112 g) butter
    1 cup (125 g) all-purpose flour
4 ½ cups (a little more than 2 L) beef broth
    2 cans or bottles (12 ounces, or 355 ml, each) stout
    1 cup (160 g) chopped onions
    1 cup (120 g) sliced carrots
    1 cup (120 g) sliced celery
    1 bag (16 ounces, or 455 g) frozen mixed vegetables
    1 can (16 ounces, or 455 g) stewed tomatoes, undrained
    ½ teaspoon salt
1 to 2 teaspoons (2 to 4 g) black pepper
    2 teaspoons (10 ml) Worcestershire sauce
    1 tablespoon (14 g) beef broth concentrate
    ¼ cup (60 g) ketchup
    2 cups (300 g) small-diced, grilled London broil

In a large, nonstick stockpot over medium heat, melt butter and stir in flour, making a bubbling paste or roux. Blend in beef broth and stout. Add onions, carrots, celery, frozen mixed vegetables, stewed tomatoes, salt, pepper, Worcestershire sauce, beef broth concentrate, ketchup, and London broil. Bring to a boil and simmer over low heat for about 40 minutes, or until vegetables are tender, stirring regularly so that vegetables don't scorch on the bottom of the stockpot.

Prep = 20 minutes   **Cook** = 45 minutes   **Yield** = 8 to 10 servings

Bulgur Salad
with Beer

This version of the classic Middle Eastern dish could be called "Southwestern Tabbouleh" because it features cilantro and cumin. For a heartier salad, toss with grilled chicken.

1 ½ cups (275 g) uncooked bulgur
1 cup (235 ml) beer, boiling hot
¼ cup (60 ml) olive oil
2 tablespoons (30 ml) lemon juice
2 teaspoons (5 g) ground cumin
1 teaspoon (2 g) black pepper
1 teaspoon (6 g) salt
4 medium tomatoes, seeded and diced
⅓ cup (55 g) minced onion
1 cup (60 g) chopped cilantro
3 tablespoons (18 g) chopped fresh mint
½ cup (50 g) sliced ripe olives

In a small bowl, pour beer over bulgur and let stand for 30 minutes. Squeeze off excess moisture. Combine olive oil, lemon juice, cumin, pepper, and salt. Toss with bulgur, along with tomatoes, onion, cilantro, mint, and olives. Chill for at least 1 hour or overnight, to blend flavors.

Prep = 15 minutes
Stand/Chill = 1 ½ to 24 hours   **Yield** = 6 servings

Beer-Battered Cajun Popcorn Shrimp Salad

Spicy beer batter is what makes popcorn shrimp a New Orleans legacy to American cuisine.

POPCORN SHRIMP:
- 1 cup (125 g) all-purpose flour, plus extra for dredging
- 1 teaspoon sweet paprika
- 2 teaspoons (3.5 g) cayenne
- 2 teaspoons (5 g) chili powder
- 1 teaspoon ground cumin
- ½ teaspoon salt
- ½ teaspoon black pepper
- 1 cup (235 ml) beer
- 1 pound (455 g) fresh shrimp, deveined
- Vegetable oil, for frying

CAJUN VINAIGRETTE:
- 3 tablespoons (45 ml) cider vinegar
- 1 clove garlic, crushed
- 3 tablespoons (45 g) Creole mustard
- 1 or 2 drops hot pepper sauce
- ½ teaspoon Worcestershire sauce
- ½ cup (120 ml) olive oil
- ½ cup (120 ml) canola oil
- Salt and black pepper

- 4 pounds (1.8 kg) mesclun

For popcorn shrimp: Combine flour with seasonings in a large bowl. Blend in beer with a wire whisk until smooth and chill for about 1 hour. Meanwhile, cut shrimp into ½-inch (1.2 cm) pieces. Preheat a deep fryer filled with oil to 375°F (190°C). Place extra flour in shallow dish. Dredge shrimp pieces lightly in flour. Dip a few pieces at a time in batter (if batter seems too thick, thin slightly with a little more beer). Fry in oil until golden and puffy. Drain on paper towels.

For vinaigrette: Whisk vinegar, garlic, and mustard until emulsified. Blend in pepper sauce and Worcestershire sauce. Slowly whisk in oils until blended, and season with salt and pepper. Toss greens with vinaigrette, and top with crisp popcorn shrimp. Serve immediately.

Prep = 35 minutes   **Cook** = 15 minutes
Chill = 1 hour   **Yield** = 4 servings

Spinach, Pear, and Apple Salad with Maple-Bacon Beer Dressing

What makes this salad novel is the pairing
of crisp apples with sweet, ripe pear slices. It's a bit
of a challenge to work out both in the produce
department and really depends on the season.
Tart green pears will ripen faster if put in
a brown bag on the kitchen counter.

1 pound (455 g) uncooked bacon
2 cups (320 g) chopped onions
½ cup (120 ml) brown ale or other beer
½ cup (120 ml) maple syrup
½ cup (120 ml) cider vinegar
1 cup (225 g) mayonnaise
3 bags (10 ounce, or 284 g each) baby spinach
3 crisp red apples, cored and sliced
2 ripe golden pears, cored and sliced
1 cup (100 g) sugar-glazed walnuts, lightly chopped

In a nonstick skillet, cook bacon until crisp, and transfer to paper
towels to drain; reserve 5 tablespoons (60 ml) drippings. Crumble
bacon when cooled and set aside. In same skillet, sauté onions in 3
tablespoons (45 ml) of reserved bacon drippings until soft and
starting to turn brown. Add ale or beer and continue cooking until
pan is deglazed and most of the liquid has evaporated. Spoon
onions into a dish and set aside. Add 2 more tablespoons (30 ml)
of bacon fat to the pan. Add maple syrup, vinegar, and mayonnaise
and blend over a low heat until smooth and melted.

Meanwhile, combine spinach, apples, and pears in a bowl. Top
with warm beer-sautéed onions. Add enough warm dressing to toss
until leaves are thoroughly coated.

Divide among serving plates and sprinkle with crumbled bacon
and chopped walnuts.

Prep = 30 minutes   **Cook** = 30 to 40 minutes
Yield = 6 to 8 servings

Fig Salad with Balsamic-Beer Dressing

Blue cheese and walnuts combine elegantly in salads. Figs, balsamic vinegar, and stout beer add a sweet-and-sour fruitiness to the composition.

BALSAMIC-BEER DRESSING:
- ½ cup (120 ml) balsamic vinegar
- ½ cup (120 ml) Guinness Stout
- 3 tablespoons (45 ml) walnut oil
- 3 tablespoons (45 ml) olive oil

SALAD:
- 16 ounces (40 g) mesclun
- 16 dried black mission figs
- ¾ cup (90 g) crumbled blue cheese
- ½ cup (60 g) toasted walnuts

For dressing: Combine vinegar and beer in a saucepan and boil until reduced by half. Blend with oils and chill for at least 3 hours. Shake well before using.

For salad: Toss greens with dressing and divide among four chilled plates. Arrange four figs on top of each salad. Sprinkle each with blue cheese and walnuts. Serve immediately.

Note: To toast walnuts: Preheat oven to 350°F (180°C, or gas mark 4) and spread walnuts on a baking sheet. Bake for 6 to 8 minutes, stirring once or twice, until evenly golden brown. Watch carefully to avoid burning.

Prep = 20 minutes   **Cook** = 10 minutes   **Chill** = 3 hours
Yield = 4 servings

Grilled Salmon Salad with Lambic-Lemon Vinaigrette

Grilled salmon makes a wonderful salad for a lunch or light supper dish. Because the salmon isn't marinated, there's little advanced prep to this dish other than having a couple of hard-boiled eggs chilled and waiting in the fridge.

LAMBIC-LEMON VINAIGRETTE:
- ⅓ cup (78 ml) lambic beer
- ⅓ cup (78 ml) fresh lemon juice
- 2 tablespoons (30 g) Dijon mustard
- 2 tablespoons (20 g) minced shallots
- 2 tablespoons (8 g) fresh dill
- Salt and pepper
- 1 cup (235 ml) light olive oil

SALMON:
- 4 salmon steaks (6 ounces, or 170 g, each)
- 1 tablespoon (15 ml) olive oil
- Salt and pepper

ASSEMBLY:
- 1 package (16 ounces, or 455 g) baby romaine lettuce
- 2 hard-cooked eggs, chilled

Prepare the vinaigrette: Combine all the vinaigrette ingredients in a medium bowl and whisk to blend.

Prepare the salmon: Brush steaks with olive oil on both sides. Season with salt and pepper. Preheat grill to medium-high and cook salmon for about 3 minutes on each side, until fish flakes easily.

To assemble salad, toss baby romaine with vinaigrette and divide among four plates. Slice each salmon steak and spread in a fan across the dressed greens. Using a cheese grater, grate hard-cooked egg over the top.

Prep = 15 minutes   **Cook** = 6 minutes
Yield = 4 servings

German Potato Salad with Biergarten Dressing

There's nothing quite like hot potato salad to serve with grilled knockwurst or bratwurst. To truly appreciate hot potato salad, it needs to be tossed with the dressing right before serving (not reheated). Simply cook the bacon and prepare the dressing ahead of time.

6 medium potatoes, peeled and cubed
½ cup (50 g) thinly sliced scallions
½ cup (60 g) diced celery
½ teaspoon salt
½ teaspoon cracked pepper
6 slices uncooked thick bacon
2 tablespoons (28 g) butter
3 tablespoons (30 g) minced onion
1 clove garlic, crushed
3 tablespoons (24 g) all-purpose flour
1 teaspoon German-style mustard
1 ¼ cups (295 ml) pilsner or lager
4 tablespoons (60 ml) cider vinegar
2 tablespoons (25 g) sugar

Cook potatoes in boiling salted water until tender and drain in a colander. Toss in a bowl with scallions, celery, salt, and pepper.

Cook bacon in a skillet until crisp and transfer bacon to paper towels to drain. Reserve bacon fat in its skillet.

Add butter to bacon fat in skillet and sauté onions and garlic until transparent. Blend in flour and mustard with a whisk and gradually whisk in beer, vinegar, and sugar. Cook, stirring constantly, until bubbling and thickened. Toss over potatoes, along with drained bacon, and serve warm.

Prep = 30 minutes   **Cook** = 35 minutes   **Yield** = 6 servings

Iceberg Raft with Beer Cheese Dressing and Bacon

After years of persona non grata status in fine restaurants, iceberg lettuce rafts have made a comeback. This 1950s staple on menus was often served with a Cheddar and blue cheese dressing. This version is spruced up with a splash of beer.

1 ¼ cups (290 g) mayonnaise
¼ cup (60 ml) beer
½ teaspoon onion salt
½ teaspoon Worcestershire sauce
½ cup (60 g) shredded sharp Cheddar cheese
½ cup (60 g) crumbled blue cheese
1 tablespoon (3 g) snipped fresh chives
1 head iceberg lettuce
⅓ cup (28 g) crisp crumbled cooked bacon

In a small bowl or glass measuring cup, blend mayonnaise, beer, onion salt, and Worcestershire sauce with a wire whisk. Stir in Cheddar cheese, blue cheese, and chives. Chill for at least 2 hours, to blend flavors. (Just before serving, a little additional beer can be stirred in if dressing seems too thick.)

Slice iceberg lettuce into four to six horizontal slabs or "rafts" (depending on size of head). Arrange on individual plates and top with dressing. Sprinkle with bacon and serve.

Prep = 15 minutes   **Chill** = 2 hours
Yield = 4 to 6 servings

Pilsner Pulled Pork
Lettuce Wraps

Every great dish deserves an encore . . . as long
as there's enough to go around. If there aren't any
leftovers, this salad is reason enough to make
pulled pork just to have some on hand.

2 cups (300 g) Pilsner Pulled Pork (page 169), chilled

⅔ cup (150 g) mayonnaise

½ cup (60 g) chopped celery

½ cup (60 g) seeded and chopped green bell pepper

¼ cup (33 g) sliced ripe olives, drained

6 large outer leaves Boston or Bibb lettuce

Combine pulled pork with mayonnaise and blend well. Mix in celery,
bell pepper, and olives. Divide pork among lettuce leaves and roll up,
securing in place with frilled toothpicks. Serve immediately or chill
for up to 1 hour.

Prep = 15 minutes   **Chill** = 0 to 1 hour
Yield = 6 wraps; 3 to 6 servings

Lee Steele's Beer-Can Chicken Salad

To make this salad, first prepare the American delicacy, Beer-Can Chicken (see page 112). It's the ultimate dish for the ultimate leftovers and makes a nice lunch on a hot summer day. Roast the corn on the grill while preparing the chicken.

BEER-CAN DRESSING:

1 ¼ cups (290 g) mayonnaise
¼ cup (60 ml) beer
1 to 2 teaspoons BBQ rub (page 109)
¼ teaspoon celery seeds
1 teaspoon (3 g) garlic powder

SALAD:

Beer-Can Chicken (page 112), fully cooked and chilled
4 ears roasted corn, chilled
1 ½ cups (180 g) diced celery
½ cup (60 g) seeded and diced red bell pepper
½ cup (60 g) seeded and diced green bell pepper
½ cup (65 g) sliced black olives
6 large leaves Boston lettuce

For dressing: Combine ingredients in a small bowl until blended.

For salad: Remove skin and bones from chicken and cut meat into cubes. Cut roasted corn from cobs. Toss chicken, corn, celery, bell peppers, and olives in a large bowl. Add enough dressing to moisten chicken to desired taste and serve in lettuce cups.

Note: To roast corn: While cooking Beer-Can Chicken, shuck ears of corn and baste lightly with olive oil. Roast for 15 to 20 minutes, turning once so that there are grill marks on both sides.

Prep = 25 minutes **Cook** = 2 hours
Chill = At least 4 hours **Yield** = 6 servings

Pasta and Pizza

Thai Chicken Pizza with Peanut Sauce

Asian-style peanut sauce has wandered its way into all types of dishes that would never have been found in the East. This pizza is among those many eclectic new creations of fusion cuisine.

PEANUT SAUCE:
- ½ cup (130 g) creamy peanut butter
- ½ cup (100 g) sugar
- 3 tablespoons (45 ml) light soy sauce
- ½ cup (120 ml) Singha beer
- 1 clove garlic, crushed
- ½ teaspoon red pepper flakes
- ½ teaspoon sesame oil

PIZZA: 2 Basic Beer Crusts (page 71)
- 2 packages (6 ounces, or 170 g, each) grilled chicken slices
- 1½ cups (75 g) bean sprouts
- 4 scallions, sliced
- ½ (62 g) cup drained, chopped water chestnuts
- 1 large carrot, grated
- 1 red bell pepper, seeded and thinly sliced
- ⅓ cup (7 g) chopped fresh cilantro
- 6 ounces (112 g) shredded mozzarella
- 6 ounces (82 g) shredded Swiss cheese

For peanut sauce: Combine peanut butter, sugar, soy sauce, beer, garlic, red pepper flakes, and sesame oil in a small saucepan, stir over medium heat until mixture is smooth and heated through. Sauce will thicken as it stands.

For pizza: Preheat oven to 400°F (200°C, or gas mark 6). Spread half of peanut sauce on each pizza crust. Top with chicken, bean sprouts, scallions, water chestnuts, carrots, bell pepper, and cilantro. Toss cheeses together and sprinkle both pizzas evenly with cheese. Bake for 10 to 15 minutes, or until crust is golden brown and cheese is bubbling hot. Serve immediately.

Prep = 30 minutes   **Cook** = 20 to 25 minutes
Yield = 2 pizzas; 4 to 8 servings

Penne with Porter, Pancetta, and Porcini Mushroom Sauce

Using both dried and fresh porcini mushrooms gives this sauce the earthy flavor you'd expect in a wild mushroom sauce. Porter gives the sauce a deep, rich color.

2 tablespoons (30 ml) extra-virgin olive oil
2 large shallots, minced
1 clove garlic, crushed
8 ounces (225 g) fresh porcini mushrooms, sliced
2 cups (570 ml) porter
2 ounces (57 g) dried porcini mushrooms, soaked in hot water
   for 30 minutes; reserve liquid
½ cup (50 g)) chopped pancetta
1 pound (454 g) penne, cooked al dente
   Salt and pepper
   Grated Parmesan cheese

In a medium nonstick skillet, sauté shallots and garlic in olive oil over medium heat until soft but not brown. And sliced mushrooms and pancetta. Continue to sauté until liquid from mushrooms has evaporated.

Add porter and the soaked dried mushrooms (with liquid) and simmer until slightly thickened. Toss mushroom sauce with pasta and season to taste with salt and pepper. Toss with grated Parmesan and serve immediately.

Prep = 20 minutes   **Cook** = 30 minutes   **Yield** = 6 servings

Beer and Bacon Bolognese Sauce

This is a rich meaty Bolognese sauce with the interesting twist of beer. If desired, you can always drain off some of the fat after browning the meat. This makes a big batch, so I like to keep a container of it in my freezer for impromptu dinners.

- 4 strips uncooked bacon
- 2 cloves garlic, crushed
- 2 cups (320 g) chopped onions
- ½ teaspoon salt
- 8 ounces (225 g) sliced mushrooms
- 1 ½ pounds (680 g) ground beef
- 1 teaspoon dried basil
- 1 teaspoon dried oregano
- 1 tablespoon (4 g) minced fresh parsley
- 2 tablespoons (30 ml) Worcestershire sauce
- 1 can (12 ounces, or 355 ml) flat beer
- 1 can (6 ounces, or 170 g) tomato paste
- 1 can (16 ounces, or 455 g) tomato puree or stewed tomatoes, undrained
- 1 cup (100 g) grated Parmesan cheese

In a large nonstick skillet, cook bacon until crisp. Stir in garlic, onions, salt, and mushrooms. Sauté over medium heat until onions and mushrooms are tender. Add beef and continue cooking until browned. (At this point, drain off some of the grease.) Add basil, oregano, parsley, Worcestershire sauce, beer, tomato paste, tomato puree, and Parmesan. Bring to a boil, then reduce heat and simmer for 30 minutes.

Prep = 10 minutes   **Cook** = 45 minutes
Yield = About 2 quarts (1.9 L), for 6 servings of pasta

Caramelized Onion, Goat Cheese, and Walnut Pizza

Caramelized onions require patience
but are well worth the effort. This pizza takes about
one hour to prepare from start to finish,
but you can't rush a good thing.

2 tablespoons (30 ml) olive oil
6 large onions, very thinly sliced
3 tablespoons (42 ml) pilsner
Salt and freshly ground black pepper
8 ounces (125 g) soft, crumbled goat cheese, such as Montrachet
²⁄₃ cup (90 g) chopped walnuts
Basic Beer Crust (page 71)

Heat oil in a large skillet or stockpot over medium heat. Add onions, pilsner, and a generous seasoning of salt and pepper. Toss well to coat, then cover the pan. Cook, tossing occasionally, until the onions are very soft and caramel brown all over. The onions need to be cooked slowly over low heat for them to caramelize properly; this will take about 45 minutes. After the first 10 minutes of cooking, you will have to lower the heat to prevent sticking. By cooking them covered, you can use less oil. Once caramelized, remove the cover from the pan, and continue cooking until golden brown and all moisture has evaporated.

After onions are cooked, preheat oven to 450°F (230°C, or gas mark 8). Spread half the onion mixture onto each pizza crust, and sprinkle each with half of the cheese. Top each pizza with walnuts.

Bake pizzas for 12 to 15 minutes, or until crust is golden and walnuts are toasted.

Prep = 15 minutes   **Cook** = 1 hour
Yield = 2 pizzas; 4 to 8 servings

Macaroni and Beer Cheese with Bacon

Adding beer and bacon to this childhood comfort-food classic turns it into a grown-up side dish or even main course pub fare. For a light supper, serve it with broiled tomatoes as a garnish and, of course, beer.

2 cups (210 g) uncooked elbow macaroni

3 tablespoons (42 g) butter

¼ cup (40 g) minced onion

2 tablespoons (16 g) all-purpose flour

½ teaspoon salt

⅛ teaspoon pepper

1 cup (235 ml) half-and-half

1 cup (235 ml) flat beer

2 cups (225 g) shredded Cheddar cheese, divided

¼ cup (20 g) crisp crumbled bacon

Cook macaroni according to package directions and drain well. In medium saucepan, melt butter over medium heat and sauté onion until tender. Blend in flour, salt, and pepper. Gradually blend in half-and-half and beer, stirring constantly with a wire whisk, until thickened. Remove from heat and blend in 1½ cups (170 g) of the cheese until melted. Combine cheese sauce with macaroni and bacon.

Preheat oven to 350°F (180°C, or gas mark 4). Spread macaroni mixture in a buttered 1½-quart (1.5 L) casserole dish, top with remaining cheese, and bake for 30 minutes, or until cheese is bubbling and golden brown.

Prep = 15 minutes   **Cook** = 1 hour   **Yield** = 4 servings

Pilsner Pasta and Pizza Sauce with Sun-Dried Tomatoes

Sun-dried tomatoes make a nice, all-purpose sauce for pasta or pizza. Let the sauce reduce to a somewhat thicker consistency or add extra tomato paste. For later use on pasta, thin with additional beer.

1 jar (12.5 ounces, or 355 g) sun-dried tomatoes, chopped, oil reserved

½ stick (4 tablespoons, or 55 g) unsalted butter

1 large green bell pepper, seeded and chopped

1 yellow onion, chopped

3 celery stalks, minced

3 carrots, minced

3 cloves garlic, minced

1 teaspoon fennel seeds

1 can (28 ounces, or 800 g) crushed tomatoes

1 can (28 ounces, or 800 g) diced tomatoes, undrained

1 to 2 tablespoons (15 to 30 g) tomato paste

1 cup (235 ml) pilsner

Salt and pepper

Heat oil from the sun-dried tomatoes and butter in a large, nonstick saucepan over medium-high heat. Add bell pepper, onion, celery, carrots, garlic, and fennel seeds. Sauté for 15 minutes, then stir in sun-dried tomatoes, crushed tomatoes, diced tomatoes, tomato paste, and pilsner. Simmer over low heat, uncovered, for 40 minutes to 1 hour, stirring often, until desired consistency. Season to taste with salt and pepper.

Prep = 20 minutes **Cook** = 1 hour to 1 hour 15 minutes
Yield = About 2 quarts (1.9 L)

Basic Beer Crust

Beer in pizza crust is a natural combination
of two great ideas. The yeast already in the beer
leavens just enough to make a unique crust, and
beer has paired perfectly with pizza since
what seems like the beginning of time.

3 cups (375 g) unbleached all-purpose flour, plus extra for dusting
1 tablespoon (13 g) sugar
1 teaspoon (4.6 g) baking powder
½ teaspoon salt
1 can or bottle (12 ounces, or 355 ml) beer (pilsner preferred)
¼ cup (60 ml) olive oil

Combine flour, sugar, baking powder, and salt in a large bowl and
mix thoroughly. Pour in beer and olive oil; mix well (dough will
be sticky). Spread a handful of flour on a work surface such as
a butcher block or marble slab, and turn out dough onto it. Toss
dough to coat it with flour and prevent it from sticking. With floured
hands, knead two or three times to make dough pliable. Shape
dough into a ball, then divide into two portions.

Preheat oven to 450°F (230°C, or gas mark 8). Grease two
baking sheets or pizza pans. Use a rolling pin to roll each ball into
an 11- or 12-inch (28 to 30 cm) circle. Fit crusts into pans or shape,
free-form, on baking sheets. Fill pizza crusts with desired toppings
and bake for 12 to 15 minutes, or until crust is golden and topping
is bubbling.

Prep = 20 minutes   **Cook** = 12 to 15 minutes
Yield = Two 11- to 12-inch (28 to 30 cm) crusts

Drunken Beer Dog Pizzas

This dish is essentially a hot dog pizza in a spicy barbecue-like sauce. The addition of bread-and-butter pickles may seem a little odd, but it's surprisingly flavorful. Alternatively, play it safe and garnish it with olives.

Basic Beer Crust (page 71)
Drunken Beer Dogs (page 22)
1 ½ cups (170 g) shredded Cheddar cheese
1 ½ cups (170 g) shredded mozzarella cheese
Bread-and-butter pickle slices, well drained and patted dry

Preheat oven to 450°F (230°C, or gas mark 8). Prepare dough for two Basic Beer Crusts and spread each with half of the prepared recipe for Barking Beer Dogs. Mix cheeses together and sprinkle evenly over both pizzas.

Top with pickle slices. Bake for 12 to 15 minutes, or until crust is golden and cheese is bubbling and starting to brown. Let cool for 5 minutes, then slice and serve immediately.

Prep = 15 minutes   **Cook** = 12 to 15 minutes
Yield = 2 pizzas; 6 to 8 servings

Porter-Cranberry-Pecan Pizza

This recipe is by definition a pizza, but it doubles as an appetizer and triples as a dessert. As if that's not enough, the porter-cranberry sauce is a great recipe for holiday festivities.

Olive oil
1 can (8 ounces, or 225 g) refrigerated crescent rolls
1 package (8 ounces, or 225 g) Brie
¾ cup (175 ml) Porter-Cranberry Sauce (recipe follows)
⅔ cup (66 g) broken pecans

Preheat oven to 425°F (220°C, or gas mark 7). Lightly brush a pizza pan with olive oil. Unroll crescent dough and use to line pan with tips facing toward the center. Press dough into pan until seams don't show. Bake for 5 to 8 minutes, or until lightly browned. Remove from oven.

Cut rind from Brie and slice into ½-inch (1.2 cm) cubes. Scatter cheese over partially baked crust. Spoon cranberry sauce by teaspoonfuls over cheese and sprinkle with pecans. Return to oven and bake for 10 minutes, or until cheese is melted and crust is golden brown. Allow to cool for 5 minutes, then slice and serve immediately.

PORTER-CRANBERRY SAUCE:
4 cups (400 g) fresh cranberries
1 cup (225 g) light brown sugar, firmly packed
1 cup (235 ml) porter

Bring cranberries, brown sugar, and porter to a boil. Simmer for about 10 minutes, or until berries pop. Let cool completely or chill. Yields about 3 ½ cups (100 g).

Prep = 15 minutes   **Cook** = 20 to 25 minutes
Yield = 8 main course or 16 appetizer/dessert servings

Portobello Mushroom, Stout, and Swiss Flatbread Pizza

Although I used Irish stout in this recipe,
the idea came originally from a Swiss-inspired veal
dish. Instead of homemade flatbread, try using
commercially prepared Indian naan—talk
about global cuisine!

  2 tablespoons (30 ml) olive oil
  8 ounces (225 g) sliced portobello mushrooms
  1 small onion, sliced
  1 cup (235 ml) Guinness Stout or porter
  1 Stout Garlic and Herb Flatbread, baked (page 214)
1 ½ cups (165 g) shredded Swiss cheese
  ½ cup (65 g) drained, sliced ripe olives

Sauté mushrooms and onions in oil in a large nonstick skillet over medium heat until tender. Add beer and continue cooking until liquid has practically evaporated. Spread mushroom mixture over flatbread and cover with cheese. Sprinkle with olives.

Preheat oven to 450°F (230°C, or gas mark 8). Bake pizza for 8 to 10 minutes, or until cheese is golden and bubbling.

Prep = 15 minutes   **Cook** = 25 to 30 minutes
Yield = 2 to 4 servings

Ham, Pineapple, and Porter Pizza

There's really nothing Italian about ham
and pineapple pizza. Why not take it one step further
away from conventional pizza? The sauce is
a simple reduction of ketchup and beer.

Basic Beer Crust (page 71)
1 ⅓ cups (320 g) ketchup
⅔ cup (156 ml) porter
2 cups (300 g) diced cooked ham
1 can (16 ounces, or 455 g) pineapple chunks,
drained very well and cut in half
3 cups (337 g) shredded white Cheddar cheese

Preheat oven to 450°F (230°C, or gas mark 8). Using Basic Beer
Crust recipe, prepare two pizza shells in pizza pans. Combine
ketchup and porter in a small saucepan over medium heat and
reduce by half, about 15 minutes. Spread over pizza crusts and top
with ham. Distribute pineapple chunks evenly over pizza.

Cover pizzas with cheese. Bake for 12 to 15 minutes, or until crust
is golden and cheese is bubbling and starting to brown. Let cool for
5 minutes. Slice and serve immediately.

Prep = 15 minutes   **Cook** = 30 minutes
Yield = 2 pizzas; 6 to 8 servings

Spaghetti Carbeernara

Nothing in this world seems to be richer than spaghetti carbonara and yet so worth every bite. This version replaces dry white wine, often used in the traditional recipe, with beer.

- 6 egg yolks
- 2 cups (475 ml) whipping cream
- ½ cup (50 g) grated Parmesan cheese
- ¼ teaspoon salt
- ¼ teaspoon pepper
- ½ pound (225 g) uncooked bacon, cut into ½-inch (1.2 cm) pieces
- ½ cup (80 g) finely diced onion
- 2 cloves garlic
- 6 ounces (half of a 12-ounce, or 355 ml, bottle) lager
- ½ teaspoon oregano
- 1 pound (455 g) dried spaghetti, cooked al dente

Combine egg yolks, cream, Parmesan cheese, salt, and pepper in a bowl and set aside. Fry bacon in a nonstick skillet until fat is released but bacon is not crispy. Pour off most of drippings and sauté onion and garlic over medium heat until soft. Add beer and oregano, and reduce until thickened. Turn off heat. Blend in cream mixture with a wire whisk until heated through. Toss with warm, well-drained spaghetti.

Prep = 15 minutes **Cook** = 30 minutes
Yield = 6 servings

Meats

Beef, Broccoli, and Beer Stir-Fry

This is one of those quick dishes you can throw together after a long day at work, when you just don't have a lot of patience to wait for dinner to happen.

1 ½ pounds (680 g) top round steak
1 can (12 ounces, or 355 ml) beer
½ cup (120 ml) strong beef broth, divided
1 teaspoon minced fresh thyme
2 teaspoons (10 ml) Mongolian fire oil
2 tablespoons (30 g) hoisin sauce
2 tablespoons (30 g) brown sugar
2 tablespoons (30 ml) cooking oil
2 cups (140 g) broccoli florets
1 cup (65 g) snow peas
1 green bell pepper, seeded and sliced
1 red bell pepper, seeded and sliced
1 yellow bell pepper, seeded and sliced
2 green apples, cored and sliced
¼ cup (32 g) cornstarch
Hot noodles or cooked wild rice

Partially freeze beef and cut meat into thin strips at an angle across the grain. Place in bowl and add beer, ¼ cup (60 ml) broth, thyme, fire oil, hoisin sauce, and brown sugar.

In a large, nonstick skillet, heat oil, add beef with sauce, and stir-fry for 2 minutes. Remove beef and set aside on plate. Add broccoli florets to skillet and stir-fry for 2 minutes. Add pea pods; green, red, and yellow peppers; and apples; stir-fry for 1 minute. Stir remaining beef broth into cornstarch and dissolve. Add cornstarch slurry to skillet and stir-fry until thickened and clear. Return seared beef to the sauce, serve over hot noodles or wild rice.

Prep = 10 minutes **Cook** = 30 to 40 minutes **Yield** = 4 servings

Osso Buco in Beer

Classic Italian osso buco is braised with stock and white wine and accented with a citrus peel mixture called *gremolada*. There are no tomatoes in authentic osso buco but many versions have adulterated it since. A pale Belgium lambic adds a nice citrus touch.

6 veal shanks, crosscut 2½ inches (6.2 cm) thick
½ teaspoon salt
¼ teaspoon pepper
¼ cup (31 g) all-purpose flour
2 tablespoons (30 ml) extra-virgin olive oil
1 can (14.5 ounces, or 411 g) diced tomatoes, undrained
1 bottle (12 ounces, or 355 ml) lambic beer
2 cloves garlic, crushed
2 teaspoons (4 g) grated lemon zest, divided
1 bay leaf
2 tablespoons (8 g) chopped fresh parsley

Sprinkle veal shanks with salt and pepper and dredge with flour. In a 4-quart (2 L) stockpot with lid, brown veal shanks in olive oil on both sides. Add tomatoes, beer, garlic, 1 teaspoon lemon zest, and bay leaf. Heat to boiling. Cover and reduce to simmer for 1½ to 2 hours. Transfer veal shanks to a serving platter. Skim fat from broth and remove bay leaf. Boil down sauce until somewhat thickened and spoon over veal shanks. Garnish with chopped parsley mixed with remaining lemon zest.

Prep = 20 minutes   **Cook** = 1 hour 40 minutes to 2 hours 10 minutes   **Yield** = 6 servings

All-American Beer Meat Loaf

The caramelized onion and beer
gravy enhance this dinnertime staple.

½ cup (50 g) herb-seasoned stuffing cubes, crushed finely
1 cup (235 ml) Miller or other domestic beer
1 ½ pounds (680 g) lean ground beef
¼ cup (40 g) minced onion
1 clove garlic, crushed
½ teaspoon salt
¼ teaspoon cracked pepper
1 teaspoon Worcestershire sauce
2 tablespoons (30 g) ketchup
1 large egg
2 strips uncooked bacon, cut in half

ONION-BEER GRAVY:
2 tablespoons (28 g) butter
1 tablespoon (15 ml) olive oil
1 large yellow onion, sliced thinly
1 tablespoon (15 g) brown sugar
1 can (12 ounces, or 355 ml) Miller or other domestic beer, divided
1 tablespoon (15 g) ketchup
1 envelope (.85 ounce, or 24 g) onion gravy mix

Preheat oven to 350°F (180°C, or gas mark 4). In a large bowl,
combine stuffing with beer. Mix in ground beef, onion, garlic, salt,
pepper, Worcestershire sauce, ketchup, and egg. Spread mixture in
an ungreased 9 × 5-inch (22.5 × 13 cm) loaf pan. Layer bacon slices
across the top of the meatloaf. Bake for 1 hour and 15 minutes.

While the meat loaf bakes, make onion-beer gravy: In a medium
nonstick skillet, sauté onion slices in butter and oil until most of the
moisture has evaporated and onions are tender. Add brown sugar
and 3 tablespoons (45 ml) of the beer. Continue cooking over
medium heat until onions are a rich, caramelized brown. Meanwhile,
combine remaining beer with ketchup and gravy mix in a glass
measuring cup. Add to pan of onions and heat through, stirring
constantly until thickened and smooth.

Let the baked meat loaf stand for 5 minutes before removing
from pan. Slice and serve with onion-beer gravy.

Prep = 25 minutes   **Cook** = 1 ½ hours   **Yield** = 6 servings

Veal Chops with Rosemary Lambic Reduction

In this recipe, substitution became the mother of invention. After running out of Chablis for my veal chops, a bottle of lambic beer was pressed into service. The result became a new recipe of choice.

1 teaspoon crushed fresh sage
1 teaspoon fresh rosemary
2 cloves garlic, crushed
1 teaspoon salt
1 teaspoon cracked pepper
2 tablespoons (30 ml) olive oil
1 tablespoon (14 g) butter
4 veal chops, 1-inch (2.5 cm) thick
1 cup (235 ml) lambic beer, divided

Combine sage, rosemary, garlic, salt, and pepper, and rub on both sides of each veal chop.

Melt butter and oil in a large nonstick skillet. Brown chops for 3 to 4 minutes on each side. Remove from skillet and pour off most of the fat. Add half of the beer to skillet. Return chops to skillet. Cover and simmer over low heat for 30 minutes. Transfer chops to a warm platter. Add remaining beer to skillet and boil down to a syrupy glaze. Pour over chops.

Prep = 10 minutes   **Cook** = 40 minutes   **Yield** = 4 servings

Asian Beer
London Broil

Many Asian beers are available these days,
mostly light to medium lagers, and any of them
suit this classic dish.

2 pounds (905 g) London broil, about 1½ to 2 inches
(3.8 to 5 cm) thick

1 can (12 ounces, or 355 ml) Asian beer

1 medium onion, sliced

1 clove garlic, crushed

¼ cup (60 ml) soy sauce

¼ cup (85 g) honey

2 teaspoons (10 ml) sesame oil

2 tablespoons (30 ml) vegetable oil

1 tablespoon (15 ml) rice vinegar

2 teaspoons (3 g) grated fresh ginger

¼ teaspoon black pepper

1 teaspoon meat tenderizer

Place steak in resealable plastic bag. Combine beer, onion, garlic, soy
sauce, honey, sesame oil, vegetable oil, vinegar, ginger, pepper, and
meat tenderizer in bowl; pour over steak. Press air out of bag and
seal securely. Refrigerate for 8 hours or overnight, turning over
occasionally. Remove steak from marinade (discard the marinade)
and place on grill 4 to 5 inches (10 to 13 cm) from coals or heat
source. Cook for 7 to 10 minutes on each side, or to desired degree
of doneness. To serve, cut across grain into thin slices.

Prep = 15 minutes   **Chill** = 8 hours   **Cook** = 14 to 20 minutes
Yield = 4 to 6 servings

Aunt BC's Pork with Porter and Turnip Greens

Turnip greens and hominy are traditional Southern fare that can now be found in supermarkets around the country. Porter adds a rich-flavored stock to this brothy stew.

1 tablespoon (15 ml) olive oil

1 boneless pork shoulder roast (3 to 4 pounds, or 1.4 to 1.8 kg)

2 bottles (12 ounces, or 355 ml, each) porter

4 cups (1 L) chicken broth

2 cloves garlic

1 teaspoon salt

1 teaspoon pepper

2 teaspoons (10 ml) Worcestershire sauce

1 large onion, cut in half

3 large celery stalks

1 package (16 ounces, or 455 g) frozen chopped turnip greens, thawed

1 can (15 ounces, or 425 g) white hominy

In a Dutch oven, brown pork shoulder on all sides in olive oil. Add porter, chicken broth, garlic, salt, pepper, Worcestershire sauce, onion, and celery. Cover tightly and bake at 350°F (180°C, or gas mark 4) for 1½ to 2 hours, or until fork tender. Remove from oven. Discard onion, celery, and garlic. Use two forks to shred the meat. Skim fat from broth and add pork back to broth. Add turnip greens and hominy. Simmer for another 20 minutes on top of the stove over low heat, uncovered.

Prep = 20 minutes **Cook** = 2 to 2 ½ hours
Yield = 6 to 8 servings

Apple Ale-Glazed Pork Chops

This is one of those simple dishes that can be thrown together with what's on hand in the refrigerator. Just about any apple-based fermented beverage will work well.

3 tablespoons (45 ml) olive oil

½ stick (4 tablespoons, or 55 g) butter, divided

4 extra-thick pork chops

Salt

2 crisp apples, cored and sliced but not peeled

1 bottle (12 ounces, or 355 ml) hard cider or apple ale

¼ cup (38 g) dark brown sugar, packed

2 tablespoons (40 g) honey

1 tablespoon (15 ml) cider vinegar

In a medium nonstick skillet, heat olive oil with 1 tablespoon (14 g) of the butter. Brown pork on both sides. Remove pork chops from pan and set aside. Melt remaining 3 tablespoons (48 g) of butter in the pan and brown apple slices over medium heat. Remove apple slices and set aside. Return pork chops to the pan along with cider, brown sugar, honey, and vinegar. Continue cooking over medium heat until liquid is reduced to a syrupy glaze. During about the last 5 minutes of cooking, add apples to the pan and heat through. Serve pork chops with apples and glaze spooned over the top.

Prep = 20 minutes   **Cook** = 10 minutes   **Yield** = 4 to 6 servings

Bock-Braised Brisket

Here is an example of a rib-sticking meal that
is elegantly simple in preparation and presentation.
The meat and vegetables are served simply au jus,
enhanced with bock, a strong, German-style
bottom-fermenting beer.

4 pounds (1.8 kg) beef brisket
1 can (12 ounces, or 355 ml) bock beer
3 tablespoons (45 ml) Worcestershire sauce
2 teaspoons (12 g) salt
1 clove garlic
8 medium potatoes
8 carrots, peeled
1 pound (455 g) pearl onions

Preheat oven to 400° F (200°C, or gas mark 6). In a large oven-proof casserole with a tight-fitting lid, brown beef, fat side down, in oven for 25 to 30 minutes. Remove meat from oven. Pour off fat and reserve. In small bowl, blend beer with Worcestershire sauce, salt, and garlic. Pour over brisket and cover tightly. Reduce heat to 350°F (180°C, or gas mark 4) and bake for 1 ½ hours. Pare strip of peel from around the center of each potato. Remove lid from casserole and add carrots, potatoes, and onions. Cover and bake for 1 hour longer, basting vegetables with broth, until vegetables are fork tender. Serve beef sliced on a platter with vegetables and broth.

Prep = 20 minutes **Cook** = 3 hours **Yield** = 8 servings

Biergarten Sauerbraten

The next time you host your own Oktoberfest, why not add some of the beer to the sauerbraten? It's a natural pairing, and the beer tenderizes the meat even more.

12 ounce (355 ml) bottle of any German lager
1 cup (235 ml) cider vinegar
½ lemon, quartered
2 bay leaves
1½ teaspoons (9 g) salt
½ teaspoon whole peppercorns
½ teaspoon whole cloves
½ teaspoon juniper berries
4 pounds (1.8 kg) lean top round
1 tablespoon (14 g) butter
1 tablespoon (8 g) flour
¼ cup (115 g) unpacked brown sugar
12 crushed gingersnaps

Combine lager, vinegar, lemon, bay leaves, salt, peppercorns, cloves, and juniper berries in a saucepan and bring to a boil. Boil 2 minutes and cool. Place roast in a glass casserole dish and pour marinade over meat. Cover with plastic wrap and refrigerate for 24 hours and up to two days, turning every 8 hours.

Remove meat and place in slow cooker. Strain marinade and pour over meat. Cook on low for 6 to 7 hours or until meat starts to fall apart around the edges. Melt butter in a 1 quart (946 ml) saucepan and blend in flour, stirring constantly to make a roux. Blend in liquid from slow cooker, along with brown sugar and gingersnaps. Cook, stirring constantly until gravy is smooth and thickened. Slice sauerbraten on platter and serve with gravy.

Prep = 20 minutes   **Cook** = 6 to 7 hours   **Yield** = 6 servings

Buffalo-Style Beer and Beef Tacos

Imagine tacos with Buffalo sauce, celery, carrots, blue cheese dressing, and beer. It's as though the classic chicken wing appetizer swung by a taco joint for inspiration.

    1 pound (455 g) lean ground beef
    ½ cup (80 g) chopped red onion
    ⅓ cup (80 g) bottled buffalo wing sauce
    ½ cup (120 ml) beer
    3 tablespoons (13 g) minced fresh cilantro
    8 taco shells
    ½ cup (60 g) chopped celery
1 ½ cups (83 g) shredded iceberg lettuce
    ½ cup (120 g) blue cheese dressing
    ½ cup (60 g) grated carrot

Sauté beef and onions in a large nonstick skillet over medium heat for 8 to 10 minutes, or until beef is browned and broken up with a spoon. Stir in buffalo wing sauce and beer. Simmer until liquid is reduced by half. Stir in cilantro. Spoon into taco shells and top with celery and lettuce. Drizzle with blue cheese dressing and garnish with grated carrot.

Prep = 30 minutes   **Cook** = 20 minutes   **Yield** = 4 servings

Filets Mignons
Beernaise

Here's a new twist on a steakhouse classic: beer is used in the tarragon-shallot reduction for béarnaise sauce. Try pairing these with Beer-Battered Onion Rings (page 178), a baked potato, and asparagus.

BEERNAISE SAUCE:
- ½ cup (120 ml) beer
- 2 tablespoons (30 ml) white wine vinegar
- 2 teaspoons (3 g) minced fresh tarragon
- 2 teaspoons (2 g) fresh minced fresh chives
- 2 tablespoons (20 g) minced shallots
- 4 egg yolks
- Juice of ½ lemon
- 1 teaspoon cold water
- 1 teaspoon salt
- 1 teaspoon ground black pepper
- 1 ½ sticks (12 tablespoons, or 337 g) soft butter

FILET MIGNON:
- 4 filet mignon (6 ounces, or 170 g each)
- Olive oil
- 1 clove garlic
- Salt and pepper

Make beer reduction for Beernaise sauce: In a small saucepan, combine beer, vinegar, tarragon, chives, and shallots. Reduce over medium heat until mixture is about 2 tablespoons (30 ml) of liquid. Let cool.

Prepare the filet mignon: Lightly coat the meat with olive oil and rub with garlic. Season with salt and pepper. Preheat a gas grill to medium-high and cook about 4 to 5 minutes on each side or until desired doneness.

While the meat cooks, finish making Beernaise sauce: In the top of a double boiler over simmering water, whisk together egg yolks, lemon juice, cold water, salt, and pepper. Add beer reduction. Gradually whisk butter into yolk mixture while cooking over simmering water. Continue whisking over low heat for 8 minutes, or until sauce is thickened. Serve immediately. If sauce breaks down, re-emulsify with a few drops of lemon juice or cold water.

Prep = 15 minutes   **Cook** = 25 minutes   **Yield** = 4 servings

Beer Beef Stroganoff

Beef stroganoff's popularity has waxed and waned over the decades. This Russian classic may as well be an American classic as well, especially when simmered in beer.

  2 tablespoons (28 g) butter
  1 tablespoon (15 ml) olive oil
  1 cup (100 g) sliced scallions
  1 clove garlic, crushed
  8 ounces (225 g) sliced mushrooms
  2 pounds (905 g) beef round steak, sliced thinly
1 ½ teaspoons (9 g) salt
  2 teaspoons (10 g) ketchup
  1 teaspoon Worcestershire sauce
  ¼ teaspoon paprika
1 ¾ cups (410 ml) flat beer, divided
  3 tablespoons (24 g) all-purpose flour
  1 cup (230 g) sour cream
    Buttered noodles or cooked wild rice

Heat butter and olive oil in a large nonstick skillet. Sauté scallions, garlic, mushrooms, and sliced round steak until meat and mushrooms are browned. Add salt, ketchup, Worcestershire sauce, paprika, and 1 ½ cups (355 ml) beer (reserve ¼ cup [55 ml]). Cover and simmer for 45 minutes. Blend together remaining beer and the flour. Blend into beef mixture, stirring constantly until mixture thickens. Blend in sour cream and heat through, but do not allow to boil or it will separate. Serve over buttered noodles or wild rice.

Prep = 15 minutes   **Cook** = 1 hour   **Yield** = 4 servings

Irish Lamb Shanks
Braised in Stout

This hearty lamb, beer, and potato
dish is humble yet elegant, like osso buco.

1 cup (125 g) all-purpose flour
1 teaspoon salt
½ teaspoon black pepper
6 lamb shanks
⅓ cup (80 ml) olive oil
12 pearl onions, peeled
3 large carrots, sliced diagonally
3 celery stalks, sliced
2 cloves garlic, crushed
½ teaspoon dried rosemary
½ teaspoon dried thyme
1 cup (235 ml) Guinness Stout
¾ cup (175 ml) beef stock
12 new potatoes, sliced in half

In a large bowl or plastic bag, combine the flour, salt, and pepper.
Add lamb shanks and dredge in flour mixture until coated. In a large
nonstick skillet over medium heat, heat the olive oil. Add lamb
shanks and cook on all sides until browned, about 10 minutes.
Transfer to a Dutch oven or ovenproof casserole. Add onions,
carrots, celery, garlic, rosemary, and thyme to the skillet and cook
for 5 minutes, stirring constantly to absorb the pan juices. Combine
the vegetables and pan juices with the lamb. Pour the Guinness and
beef stock over lamb and vegetables. Bring to a boil, reduce heat,
then cover. Simmer for 1 hour and 15 minutes. Add potatoes, place
lid back on pan, and cook for another hour, until meat is tender. To
serve, place each lamb shank in the middle of a broad soup bowl
and spoon vegetables and broth around the shank.

Prep = 20 minutes   **Cook** = 2 ½ hours   **Yield** = 6 servings

Pork Ribs in Sauerkraut and Beer

Here's a classic Midwestern (U.S.) dish with German roots. Just about any type of beer will lend its own unique flavor nuances. This is a perfect dish for experimenting with craft beers.

1 bag (16 ounces, or 455 g) sauerkraut, rinsed and drained
½ teaspoon caraway seeds
1 onion, chopped
2 red-skinned apples, cored and sliced (do not peel)
2 to 3 pounds (905 g to 1.4 kg) country-style pork ribs
1 cup (235 ml) beer

Mix sauerkraut with caraway seeds, onion, and apple. Spread on bottom of a slow cooker and layer ribs on top. Pour beer over ribs. Cover and cook on low setting for 8 to 10 hours.

Serve pork chops over a bed of sauerkraut on a large platter or on individual plates.

Prep = 15 minutes   **Cook** = 8 to 10 hours   **Yield** = 4 to 6 servings

Pilsner-Glazed Pork Chops with Pineapple-Cilantro Salsa

Pineapple salsa pairs well with nearly any kind of meat or seafood dish. These pork chops have both Asian inspiration and a Latin-American accent.

PORK CHOP MARINADE:

- 6 ounces (half of a 12-ounce, or 355 ml bottle) pilsner
- 1 teaspoon grated fresh ginger
- ½ teaspoon curry powder
- ½ teaspoon allspice
- 3 tablespoons (42 g), packed dark brown sugar
- 2 tablespoons (30 ml) Worcestershire sauce
- 2 cloves garlic, crushed
- 2 tablespoons (30 ml) lime juice

- 6 lean boneless pork chops (¾-inch [1.8 cm] -thick)

PILSNER GLAZE:

- 6 ounces (half of a 12-ounce, or 355 ml, bottle) pilsner
- ¼ cup (62 g) hoisin sauce
- 2 tablespoons (28 g) light brown sugar, packed
- 2 tablespoons (30 ml) soy sauce
- ¼ cup (75 g) plum preserves
- 1 teaspoon grated fresh ginger

PINEAPPLE-CILANTRO SALSA:

- 2 cups (300 g) finely chopped fresh pineapple
- ⅔ cup (98 g) seeded and diced red bell pepper
- ⅔ cup (110 g) finely chopped red onion
- 3 tablespoons (12 g) finely chopped cilantro leaves
- ¼ teaspoon salt
  Grated zest of 1 lime
- 2 tablespoons (30 ml) lime juice
  Dash of hot pepper sauce
- 1 tablespoon (15 ml) olive oil

For pork chop marinade: Combine beer, ginger, curry, allspice, brown sugar, Worcestershire sauce, garlic, and lime juice in a glass measuring cup. Place pork chops in a glass baking dish and pour marinade over meat. Cover and refrigerate for 2 hours. Turn meat over, cover, and chill for another 2 hours.

For pilsner glaze: Bring all of the ingredients to a boil in a small saucepan and reduce heat. Simmer to a reduction of half or until glaze is thick and syrupy.

On a grill heated to medium-high, cook pork chops (discard marinade) for 8 to 10 minutes on each side while brushing with pilsner glaze during the last half of cooking. Brush finished pork chops with pilsner glaze and serve with pineapple-cilantro salsa.

For pineapple-cilantro salsa: Combine salsa ingredients in medium bowl. Cover and let stand for at least 30 minutes to blend flavors. Serve chilled or at room temperature.

Prep = 35 minutes   **Chill** = 4 hours
Cook = 30 to 40 minutes   **Yield** = 6 servings

Pilsner
Shepherd's Pie

True shepherd's pie is made with
lamb, although most versions today use beef.
(It can even be made with turkey.) Dabble with beers
by substituting a pilsner with a porter or stout.

2 pounds (905 g) ground lamb or beef
  Salt and pepper
1 carrot, peeled and chopped
1 onion, chopped
½ cup (60 g) minced celery
½ stick (4 tablespoons, or 55 g) butter
¼ cup (31 g) all-purpose flour
1 cup (235 ml) beef broth
1 cup (235 ml) pilsner
2 teaspoons (10 ml) Worcestershire sauce
1 cup (130 g) frozen peas
  Pilsner Mashed Potatoes with Parsley, Chives,
  and Cheddar Cheese (page 182)
  Paprika
½ cup (60 g) shredded Cheddar cheese

Season meat with salt and pepper. Sauté meat in a large skillet until
it is brown and crumbly. (If you are using lamb, the pan may be too
fatty, so spoon away some of the drippings.) Add chopped carrot,
onion, and celery to the meat. Sauté with meat for 5 minutes, stirring frequently. In a medium saucepan, melt butter over medium
heat and blend in flour. Cook, blending constantly until a bubbling
paste or roux. Whisk in beef broth, pilsner, and Worcestershire
sauce. Let gravy cook and thicken for 1 minute. Add gravy to meat
and vegetables. Stir in peas.

Preheat broiler to high. Fill an ovenproof casserole with meat mixture. Spoon potatoes evenly over meat. Sprinkle potatoes with
paprika and top with shredded cheese. Broil 6 to 8 inches (15 to 20
cm) from the heat until potatoes are evenly browned.

Prep = 20 minutes   **Cook** = 25 to 30 minutes
Yield = 6 to 8 servings

Porc à la Flemande

This being a traditional Flemish dish,
using a Belgian-style white beer (witbier) is perfectly
appropriate. Wheat, coriander, and orange are added
during the brewing process. The new potatoes
can be roasted concurrently and then
added to the stew.

1 tablespoon (15 ml) olive oil

2 pounds (905 g) pork shoulder, cut into cubes

Salt and pepper

2 ½ cups (570 ml) Blue Moon beer

1 can (14 ounces, or 425 ml) chicken broth

1 teaspoon dried rosemary

2 celery stalks

1 bag (16 ounces, or 455 g) frozen pearl onions

1 package (16 ounces, or 455 g) cooked baby carrots

½ stick (4 tablespoons, or 55 g) butter

¼ cup (31 g) all-purpose flour

Roasted new potatoes

Heat olive oil over medium heat in a large nonstick skillet or saucepan with a tight-fitting cover. Add pork cubes and sprinkle with a little salt and pepper. Brown cubes on all sides. Add beer, chicken broth, rosemary, and celery. Cover and simmer for 45 minutes. Add onions and carrots; simmer for 30 minutes longer. In a small saucepan over medium heat, melt butter with flour to make a bubbling paste or roux. Add to stew mixture and blend in until thickened. Stir in roasted new potatoes and serve.

Note: To roast potatoes: Slice a dozen new potatoes in half and toss in a bowl with 1 tablespoon (15 ml) of olive oil until well coated. Preheat oven to 400°F (200°C, or gas mark 6). Line a baking sheet with aluminum foil and brush with a little additional olive oil. Place potatoes on foil, cut side down, and lightly sprinkle with salt. Bake for 30 to 40 minutes, or until tender and cut sides are golden brown.

Prep = 15 minutes   **Cook** = 1 hour 25 minutes
Yield = 6 to 8 servings

Slow-Cooked Knockwurst and Cabbage in Pilsner

Pilsner is the beer of choice when cooking cabbage. The recipe is particularly efficient because it can all be placed in a slow cooker for hands-free preparation.

 8 knockwursts
 2 teaspoons (10 ml) olive oil
 1 head green cabbage, sliced ¼-inch (6 mm) thick
 ½ cup (60 g) thinly sliced yellow onion
 2 teaspoons (4 g) caraway seeds
 ½ teaspoon salt
 2 cups (475 ml) pilsner
 2 cups (475 ml) chicken broth
 ¼ cup (30 g) minced fresh parsley (optional)

Cut knockwursts into thirds on the diagonal. Heat olive oil in non-stick skillet and brown sausages on all sides. Transfer to a 4 ½-quart (2 L) slow cooker. Add cabbage and onions. Sprinkle with caraway seeds and salt. Pour beer and chicken broth over contents of casserole. Cover and cook on low setting for 4 hours, or cook on high setting for 2 hours. Stir in parsley during the last 30 minutes of cooking.

Prep = 10 minutes   **Cook** = 2 hours (on high setting), 4 hours (on low setting)   **Yield** = 8 servings

Pork Stir-Fry with Bell Peppers Porter

Last-minute dinners can sometimes be a challenge, but this recipe is ready in no time flat. Porter beer and Asian-flair seasoning has a healthy dose of East meets West in this fusion-style dish.

1 tablespoon (15 ml) olive oil
1 pound (455 g) boneless pork loin or leg, cut into cubes
1 clove garlic, crushed
1 medium red bell pepper, seeded and sliced
1 medium green bell pepper, seeded and sliced
½ cup (120 ml) porter
2 cups (130 g) fresh snow peas
⅓ cup (80 g) bottled stir-fry sauce
3 tablespoons (45 g) black bean sauce
Steamed rice

Heat olive oil over medium-high heat in a large nonstick skillet or wok. Stir-fry pork cubes until browned. Add garlic and peppers, and stir-fry for another minute. Add porter and bring to a boil. Stir in snow peas and continue cooking on high until almost all of the liquid has evaporated. Stir in stir-fry sauce and black bean sauce. Heat through and serve over rice.

Prep = 15 minutes   **Cook** = 24 minutes   **Yield** = 4 servings

Skillet Steaks with Porter and Peppercorn Sauce

Shell steaks are the geographically neutral term for the traditional Kansas City steaks (as opposed to New York strip steaks). Try using porter as a new spin on peppercorn cream sauce.

PEPPERCORN CREAM SAUCE:

1 bottle (12 ounces, or 355 ml) porter
1 teaspoon cracked black pepper
1 ounce (1 tablespoon, or 15 ml) whiskey
1 cup (235 ml) heavy cream

STEAKS:

4 shell steaks (6 ounces, or 170 g each)
Salt and cracked black pepper
1 tablespoon (14 ml) olive oil
1 clove garlic, minced
1 teaspoon minced shallot
1 cup (70 g) baby bella mushrooms, sliced
1 ounce (1 tablespoon, or 15 ml) whiskey
1 teaspoon Dijon mustard

For peppercorn cream sauce: In a small saucepan over medium heat, combine beer, cracked black pepper, whiskey, and cream. Simmer until reduced to 1 cup (235 ml), stirring frequently. Remove from heat and set aside.

For steaks: Season steaks with salt and pepper. In a medium non-stick skillet, heat olive oil, garlic, and shallots for 1 minute. Stir in mushrooms and sauté until tender. Remove mushroom mixture from pan and set aside. Add steaks to skillet (with a little additional olive oil, if necessary) and cook on each side for about 4 minutes, or until desired doneness. Deglaze skillet with whiskey and return mushroom mixture to pan along with peppercorn cream sauce and Dijon mustard. Reduce until sauce is thickened, and pour over steaks.

Prep = 15 minutes   **Cook** = 25 minutes   **Yield** = 4 servings

Sloppy Drunk Joes

Even a simple sandwich like sloppy joes can be punched up with a can of beer. These are sure to be a hit. Lagers, ales, porters, or stouts—it doesn't matter which you choose, they all create the same effect.

1 pound (455 g) lean ground beef
¼ cup (40 g) chopped onion
¼ cup (37 g) seeded and chopped green bell pepper
½ teaspoon garlic powder
1 teaspoon prepared yellow mustard
1 cup (240 g) ketchup
1 cup (235 ml) beer
1 tablespoon (15 g) brown sugar
   Salt and pepper
4 toasted hamburger buns

In a medium nonstick skillet, brown beef , onion, and green bell pepper. Drain off any fat. Stir in garlic powder, mustard, ketchup, beer, and brown sugar. Reduce heat and simmer for 30 to 40 minutes, or until liquid is reduced to a thick sauce, stirring occasionally. Season with salt and pepper to taste and serve on buns.

Prep = 10 minutes   **Cook** = 40 to 50 minutes   **Yield** = 4 servings

Steak and Stout Pie

This is the traditional style of beef pot pie you'll find all over in the pubs of England and Ireland. Any stout or porter style of beer produces a rich, brown gravy.

1 tablespoon (15 ml) olive oil
1 tablespoon (14 g) butter, plus 2 tablespoons (28 g), softened
1 pound (455 g) round steak, cut into cubes
1 clove garlic, crushed
1 cup (160 g) chopped onion
8 ounces (225 g) mushrooms, sliced
1 bottle (12 ounces, or 355 ml) Guinness Stout
1 can (12 ounces, or 355 ml) condensed beef broth
1 teaspoon salt
½ teaspoon black pepper
½ teaspoon paprika
¼ teaspoon dried marjoram
¼ teaspoon dried thyme
8 new potatoes, quartered
¼ cup (31 g) all-purpose flour
Pastry for a 9-inch (23 cm) single-crust pie

In a large nonstick skillet with a tight-fitting lid, sauté steak cubes in olive oil and 1 tablespoon (14 g) butter until nicely browned. Add garlic, onions, and mushrooms, and continue to cook until moisture has evaporated from mushrooms and onions and they are tender. Add stout and beef broth, salt, pepper, paprika, marjoram, and thyme. Cover and simmer for 40 minutes. Add new potatoes, cover, and simmer for 30 minutes longer.

Blend together softened butter and flour. Add to broth mixture and blend until liquid thickens and comes to a boil. Pour into a buttered casserole or 9-inch (23 cm) deep-dish pie plate or ceramic quiche pan. Cover with pastry, crimp edges, and cut slits for steam to vent.

Preheat oven to 400°F (200°C, or gas mark 6). Bake pie for 30 to 40 minutes, until crust is golden.

Prep = 35 minutes   **Cook** = 2 hours   **Yield** = 4 to 6 servings

Stout and Spicy
Pork Satay

There's something about stout that enhances peanut butter in recipes. This makes a great appetizer or entrée, depending on portion size.

1 pound (455 g) pork tenderloin
3 stalks lemongrass
1 tablespoon (8 g) grated fresh ginger
2 cloves garlic, crushed
1 onion
2 teaspoons (4 g) ground fennel
2 teaspoons (5 g) ground cumin
2 teaspoons (4 g) ground coriander
1 teaspoon ground turmeric
1 tablespoon (15 ml) lime juice
1 tablespoon (15 ml) peanut oil
¼ cup (60 ml) stout
½ teaspoon salt
½ teaspoon black pepper
12 10-inch (26 cm) bamboo skewers
   (presoaked in water for 30 minutes)

PEANUT SAUCE:
1 cup (260 g) peanut butter
2 cloves garlic, crushed
1 tablespoon (8 g) grated fresh ginger
1 teaspoon ground turmeric
½ teaspoon Tabasco
1 tablespoon (15 g) toasted sesame oil
4 tablespoons (60 ml) soy sauce
2 tablespoons (40 g) honey
   Juice of 1 lemon
½ cup (120 ml) stout

Slice pork tenderloin against the grain, ¼-inch (6 mm) thick and 4 to 6 inches (10 to 15 cm) long. Thread onto presoaked skewers.

Remove tough outer leaves of lemongrass and discard. Chop inner parts of stalks. Place in food processor with ginger, garlic, onion, fennel, cumin, coriander, turmeric, lime juice, peanut oil, beer, salt, and black pepper. Blend to form a paste. Spread paste over both sides of kabobs. Cover and refrigerate for at least 4 hours or up to 24 hours. Grill for 3 minutes on each side, and serve with peanut sauce.

For peanut sauce: Combine ingredients in blender and pulse until smooth. Cover and let stand for at least 30 minutes, for flavors to blend.

Prep = 35 minutes   **Chill** = 4 to 24 hours
Cook = 6 to 12 minutes   **Yield** = 4 to 8 servings

Poultry

Turkey with Beer and Black-Eyed Peas

Next time there is leftover turkey, use some comfort-food inspiration for a casserole. This dish combines lentils, black-eyed peas, and beer, topped off with a crunchy topping of corn-bread stuffing.

　6 slices uncooked bacon, cut into ½-inch (1.2 cm) pieces
　½ cup (65 g) chopped carrot
　½ cup (60 g) chopped celery
　½ cup (80 g) chopped onion
　1 cup (192 g) dried lentils, sorted and rinsed
　1 can (14.5 ounces, or 451 g) Italian-style stewed tomatoes, undrained
　1 can (15 ounces, or 425 g) black-eyed peas, drained and rinsed
　3 tablespoons (11 g) minced fresh parsley
　¼ teaspoon dried thyme
　¼ teaspoon dried marjoram
　1 bottle or can (12 ounces, or 355 ml) lager
　½ cup (120 ml) condensed chicken broth
　½ cup (140 g) chili sauce
　1 teaspoon Worcestershire sauce
　2 cups (455 g) cubed turkey
　1 ⅓ cups (153 g) lightly crushed corn-bread stuffing
　3 tablespoons (42 g) butter, melted
　Nonstick cooking spray, for casserole

In a large nonstick skillet, sauté bacon, carrots, celery, and onions for 3 to 5 minutes, or until vegetables are tender-crisp. Add lentils and sauté for about 3 minutes longer. Stir in tomatoes, black-eyed peas, parsley, thyme, marjoram, beer, chicken broth, chili sauce, and Worcestershire sauce and turkey. Spray 3-quart (1.5 kg) glass baking dish with nonstick cooking spray. Spoon mixture into baking dish.

Preheat oven to 350°F (180°C, or gas mark 4). Cover casserole with aluminum foil and bake for 1 hour. Meanwhile, mix cornbread stuffing with melted butter. After 1 hour, remove foil cover and sprinkle casserole with cornbread stuffing. Bake for an additional 10 minutes, or until liquid is mostly absorbed and topping is lightly browned.

Prep = 30 minutes　**Cook** = 1 hour 20 minutes　**Yield** = 6 servings

Apple Ale-Honey Mustard Chicken Drumsticks

Slashing drumsticks helps the marinade flavor the meat as well as ensure quicker cooking. Try a ciderlike apple ale in this recipe, but any beer you have on hand will do.

8 chicken drumsticks

3 cloves garlic, crushed

⅓ cup (113 g) honey

1 tablespoon (16 g) brown mustard

2 tablespoons (30 ml) soy sauce

1 bottle (12 ounces, or 355 ml) apple ale

1 tablespoon (15 ml) cider vinegar

1 tablespoon (15 ml) olive oil

Using poultry shears, cut three gashes in the side of each chicken leg. Place drumsticks in an 8-inch (20 cm) square glass baking pan. Combine garlic, honey, mustard, soy sauce, apple ale, vinegar, and olive oil in a glass measuring cup. Pour marinade over drumsticks and cover with plastic wrap. Refrigerate for 6 hours, turning once.

Heat grill to medium-high. Grill drumsticks for a total of 15 to 18 minutes, turning every 3 minutes, until chicken is opaque with no trace of pink at the bone.

Prep = 15 minutes   **Chill** = 6 hours
Cook = 15 to 18 minutes   **Yield** = 4 servings

Artichoke Chicken Thighs in Beer

Boneless, skinless chicken thighs offer an infusion of flavor, if you're getting tired of white meat chicken breasts, which tend to be drier. The Mediterranean preparation makes this dish even more heart healthy.

4 tablespoons (65 ml) olive oil, divided
1 cup (70 g) porcini mushrooms, sliced
2 cloves garlic, peeled and halved
1 pound (455 g) boneless, skinless chicken thighs
Salt and freshly ground black pepper
2 tablespoons (3.4 g) fresh rosemary, chopped
¼ teaspoon crushed red pepper flakes
1 cup (240 ml) beer
14 ounce (397 g) artichokes, rinsed well, drained, and cut in half
12 cherry tomatoes
12 pitted ripe olives, halved

In a large, nonstick skillet, heat 2 tablespoons (33 ml) of olive oil over medium heat and sauté mushrooms and garlic until tender; set aside. Add remaining olive oil to pan. Season the chicken thighs with salt and pepper, and brown on all sides. Add rosemary, pepper flakes, beer, and mushrooms. Cover and simmer on low for about an hour. Add artichokes, tomatoes, and olives to chicken, and heat through before serving.

Prep = 15 minutes   **Cook** = 1 hour and 15 minutes
Yield = 4 servings

American Classic
Beer-Can Chicken

This is nothing short of a cult classic.
Essentially, a can of beer is nestled into the
cavity of a capon, and the can functions as a third
"leg." It gets tricky—it can fall on its side if one is not
careful. (Entrepreneurs have invented gadgets
that allow beer-can chicken to roast
while preventing such mishaps!)

1 whole chicken (3½ to 4 pounds, or 1.4 to 1.8 kg)

2 teaspoons (10 ml) olive oil

¼ cup (56 g) BBQ Rub (recipe follows),
or a similar commercial product

1 can (12 ounces, or 355 ml) beer

1 clove garlic

Wash chicken inside and out and pat dry with paper towels. Rub
the outside of chicken with olive oil. Rub the BBQ seasoned rub on
the outside and in the cavity of chicken. Wrap in plastic wrap and
refrigerate for 1 hour.

Preheat a covered grill to 375°F to 400°F (190°C to 200°C). (If
using wood chips, such as hickory or mesquite, soak them in beer.)
If your grill has three burners, just heat the two on the outside, not
the one in the middle. If your grill only has two burners, heat only
one.

Remove plastic wrap from chicken. Pour out about 1 inch (2.5 cm)
of beer from the top of the can and push a garlic clove down into
the can of beer. Stand the chicken on the can of beer by inserting
it snugly over the open can and tuck under wing tips. Place on the
grill over the unlit burner. The legs and the can should balance like
a tripod. Cover and cook for 2 hours.

BBQ RUB:

¼ cup (72 g) sea salt

¼ cup (28 g) paprika

¼ cup (60 g) brown sugar, firmly packed

2 tablespoons (12 g) black pepper

1 teaspoon dry mustard

Combine ingredients and store in an airtight jar.

Prep = 10 minutes   **Cook** = 2 hours   **Chill** = 1 hour
Yield = 4 to 6 servings

Rawleigh's Curried Beer-Can Chicken

Rawleigh Morse of Connecticut is a beer-can chicken fan and developed this curried version of the American classic. She uses a special beer-can chicken pan in which the beer is poured first into a chamber. It can be baked in the oven or roasted on a grill. For preparing the dish without the special pan, refer to American Classic Beer-Can Chicken on the opposite page.

½ cup (50 g) curry powder
½ cup (95 g) Lawry's seasoned salt
1 tablespoon (7 g) ground cinnamon
1 teaspoon (2.7 g) grated nutmeg
2 tablespoons (12 g) ground pepper
1 (12 ounces, or 355 ml) can beer
1 whole chicken (3 pounds, or 1.4 kg)

Combine all seasonings in a bowl. Mix 2 to 3 tablespoons (24 to 36 g) of the seasoning into the beer. At this point, it is poured into the pan chamber. Alternatively, pour 1 inch (2.5 cm) of beer out of can, add the 2 tablespoons (24 to 36 g) seasoning to the beer, and refer to directions for standing without a pan on page 112. Rub remaining seasoning all over chicken, making sure to lift up the skin of the chicken to coat the breast.

Preheat oven or grill to 375°F (190°C, or gas mark 5). Cook for 45 to 50 minutes, or until an internal thermometer reads 175°F (79.5°C). Let stand for 10 minutes before carving.

Prep = 10 minutes   **Cook** = 45 minutes to 1 hour   **Chill** = 1 hour
Yield = 4 to 6 servings

Caribbean Slow-Cooked Chicken

Jerk seasoning is what gives this dish its trademark flavor, along with a popular imported Jamaican lager that can be found on many supermarket shelves.

2 large sweet potatoes, peeled and cut into 2-inch (2.5 cm) pieces
1 cup (130 g) thinly sliced Vidalia onion
1 cup (165 g) golden raisins, packed
1 can (20 ounce, or 568 g) pineapple tidbits, drained
1 large ripe mango, peeled, pitted, and diced
4 boneless, skinless chicken breasts
4 teaspoons (20 g) Jamaican Jerk seasoning (page 131)
1 cup (235 ml) Red Stripe beer or other lager
2 tablespoons (30 g) dark brown sugar, firmly packed
3 tablespoons (24 g) grated fresh ginger
2 tablespoons (30 ml) Worcestershire sauce
2 teaspoons (4 g) grated lime zest
2 teaspoons (4 g) grated orange zest
1 teaspoon cumin seeds, crushed

Place sweet potatoes on bottom of slow cooker and cover with onions, raisins, drained pineapple, and mango cubes. Coat chicken breasts with jerk seasoning and place over potato mixture. Combine beer, brown sugar, ginger, Worcestershire sauce, lime zest, orange zest, and cumin seeds. Pour liquid over chicken. Cook on low setting for 7 to 9 hours or on high setting for 3 to 4 hours. (Check pot about every 2 hours, and if too much liquid evaporates, add more beer.) Serve chicken with potato mixture. Spoon reamining glaze from the slow cooker over chicken breasts.

Prep = 25 minutes   **Cook** = 3 to 4 hours (on high setting),
7 to 9 hours (on low setting)   **Yield** = 4 servings

Chicken Beerkabobs

Beer naturally tenderizes chicken and helps
it brown on the grill. Use your imagination and vary
the marinade from a light lager to a hearty ale or
stout—whatever you have in the fridge!

¼ cup (60 ml) olive oil, plus extra for grill
2 tablespoons (30 ml) balsamic vinegar
3 tablespoons (45 g) dark brown sugar, firmly packed
Juice of 1 lime
1 (12 ounces, or 355 ml) can beer
½ teaspoon salt
¼ teaspoon black pepper
2 teaspoons (5 g) chili powder
¼ teaspoon cayenne
½ teaspoon paprika
½ teaspoon onion powder
2 cloves garlic, crushed
2 teaspoons (10 ml) Worcestershire sauce
1 pound (455 g) boneless, skinless chicken breasts, cut into cubes
Button mushrooms
Bell pepper slices
Fresh baby corn
Wooden grilling skewers, presoaked in water for 30 minutes

Blend together ¼ cup (60 ml) olive oil, vinegar, brown sugar, lime
juice, beer, salt, black pepper, chili powder, cayenne, paprika, onion
powder, garlic, and Worcestershire sauce in a bowl. Place chicken in
a resealable plastic bag, cover with half of the marinade, and
refrigerate for 4 hours, reserving the other half of the marinade
separately. Remove chicken from marinade, (discard marinade),
and thread on skewers, alternating with mushrooms, bell peppers,
and baby corn. Place in a baking dish and cover with the reserved
marinade. Cover with plastic and refrigerate for 2 or 3 more hours.

Lightly oil grill and preheat to medium-high. Grill kebabs for about
15 minutes, turning once or twice, or until juices in chicken run clear.

Prep = 25 minutes   **Chill** = 6 or 7 hours
Cook = 15 minutes   **Yield** = 4 servings

Framboise Lambic-Glazed Duckling

Lambic beers are often produced with wonderful essences of fruit. Framboise is the perfect pairing for a glazed duckling. Stir in fresh raspberries at the last minute so they'll heat through without cooking.

2 ducklings (3 ½ pound, or 1.6 kg each)
Salt

SAUCE:
1 bottle (12 ounces, or 355 ml) Framboise Lambic
1 jar (12 ounce, or 340 g) seedless raspberry preserves
2 tablespoons (28 g) butter
1 cup (125 g) fresh raspberries

Cooked wild rice or mashed sweet potatoes

Preheat oven to 350°F (180°C, or gas mark 4). Remove neck and giblets from cavities of ducks. Fold wing tips under wings and fasten neck skin to duckling with back of a skewer. Pierce skin of ducks all over and lightly sprinkle with salt. Place ducks breast side up in a roasting pan. Roast, uncovered, 2 to 2 ½ hours, until crisp. Cool slightly.

Meanwhile, prepare sauce: Bring beer, raspberry preserves, and butter to a boil in a medium saucepan and reduce at a slow boil until it is a syrupy glaze that coats a spoon. Set aside on top of stove.

Split ducks in half and remove rib bones, leaving leg and wing bones intact. Place duck halves skin side up on roasting pan rack. Return to oven for 8 to 15 minutes longer, to recrisp skin. Blend raspberries into warm glaze and spoon sauce over duck halves on plates. Serve with wild rice or mashed sweet potatoes.

Prep = 20 minutes   **Cook** = 2¾ to 3 hours   **Yield** = 4 servings

Coq au Lager

This recipe is nothing more than a takeoff of
the French classic coq au vin. Just about any type of
beer can be used, even a hearty stout or porter.
The character of the dish changes according
to the beer you use.

½ cup (63 g) all-purpose flour
1 teaspoon salt
¼ teaspoon pepper
1 chicken (3½ pounds, or 1.6 kg), cut up
6 strips uncooked bacon, cut across into thin strips
8 ounces (225 g) sliced baby bella mushrooms
1 package (10 ounces, or 280 g) frozen pearl onions
2 medium carrots, sliced
2 medium parsnips, sliced
1 clove garlic, crushed
½ cup (120 ml) chicken broth
1 can or bottle (12 ounces, or 355 ml) Coors beer
2 large celery stalks, sliced
1 bouquet garni

In a small dish, mix flour with salt and pepper. Dredge chicken in
flour. In a large skillet over medium heat, fry bacon until crisp and
remove with a slotted spoon to drain on paper towels, reserving the
fat in the pan. Brown chicken in bacon fat, turning on all sides until
even in color, about 15 minutes. Remove chicken from pan and add
mushrooms and onions, stirring and cooking until mushrooms are
tender.

Drain all fat from skillet. Add chicken back to mushrooms and
onions, along with carrots, parsnips, garlic, chicken broth, and beer.
Add celery and bouquet garni. Cover and simmer for 40 to 45 minutes, or until chicken is tender.

To make bouquet garni: Combine 2 bay leaves, 4 parsley sprigs, 1
teaspoon dried thyme, and 1 teaspoon dried marjoram in a cheesecloth and tie with kitchen string.

Prep = 25 minutes   **Cook** = 1 hour 20 to 30 minutes
Yield = 6 servings

Corn Bread–Crusted Chicken Pot Pie with Pilsner and Artichokes

This version of chicken pot pie is so easy because it sidesteps the pie crust, which always gets soggy during baking. The corn bread batter is dropped by the spoonful over the filling.

1 tablespoon (15 g) olive oil

1 pound (455 g) boneless, skinless chicken breasts, cut into cubes

½ to 1 teaspoon peppered seasoned salt

1 clove garlic, crushed

2 shallots, chopped

½ cup (60 g) diced celery

½ cup (75 g) seeded and diced red bell pepper

2 cups (140 g) sliced mushrooms

1 cup (235 ml) pilsner

½ teaspoon dried thyme

1 package (10 ounces, or 280 g) frozen peas and carrots, thawed and drained

1 package (10 ounces, or 280 g) frozen artichokes, cooked and well drained

⅓ cup (75 g) butter

⅓ cup (41 g) all-purpose flour

1 ¼ cups ((295 ml) chicken broth

1 ¾ cups (410 ml) half-and-half

Salt and pepper

Nonstick cooking spray, for casserole

1 tablespoon (5 g) grated Parmesan cheese

CORN BREAD CRUST:

1 pouch (6.5 ounces, or 185 g) corn muffin mix

⅓ cup (78 ml) milk

1 egg

2 tablespoons (28 g) butter, melted

In a large nonstick skillet, heat olive oil over medium-high heat and sauté chicken with peppered seasoned salt, garlic, shallots, celery, bell pepper, and mushrooms until chicken is opaque and mushrooms are tender. Add beer and reduce mixture until almost all liquid has evaporated. Remove from heat. Stir in peas and carrots and artichokes.

Meanwhile, melt butter in a large nonstick saucepan. Blend in flour and salt and cook over medium heat until mixture is smooth and bubbling. Blend in chicken broth and half-and-half and cook, stirring constantly, until sauce thickens and is smooth and bubbling. Stir into chicken mixture. Adjust seasoning with salt and pepper. Spray a 9 × 13-inch (22.5 × 32.5 cm) casserole with nonstick cooking spray and spoon chicken mixture into it.

For corn bread crust, stir together corn bread mix, milk, egg, and melted butter in a bowl, just until combined.

Preheat oven to 400°F (200°C, or gas mark 6). Drop corn bread mixture over the top of chicken casserole by large spoonfuls. Sprinkle with Parmesan cheese. Bake for 20 to 22 minutes, until crust is brown. Let stand for 5 minutes before serving.

Prep = 30 minutes   **Cook** = 40 minutes   **Yield** = 6 servings

Country-Fried Chicken with Beer Gravy

Pan-fried chicken is a dying art in many restaurants, as it is so much easier to resort to a fast fix with the deep fryer. This recipe is inspired from a classic dish. The beer in the pan gravy is a new twist. As always, mashed potatoes are a must.

1 ½ cups (355 ml) milk, divided
1 egg, beaten
1 cup (125 g) all-purpose flour
2 teaspoons (6 g) garlic salt
1 teaspoon paprika
1 teaspoon ground black pepper
¼ teaspoon poultry seasoning
1 chicken (4 pounds, or 1.8 kg), cut up
3 cups (710 ml) vegetable oil
1 cup (235 ml) beer
1 cup (235 ml) half-and-half

In a medium bowl, beat together ½ cup (120 ml) milk and the egg. In a resealable plastic bag, mix together the flour, garlic salt, paprika, pepper, and poultry seasoning. Place chicken in bag, seal, and shake to coat. Remove chicken and dip in milk and egg mixture, then once more in flour mixture. Reserve any remaining flour mixture.

In a large nonstick skillet, heat oil to 365°F (185°C). Place coated chicken in the hot oil and brown on all sides. Reduce heat to medium-low and continue cooking chicken until tender, about 30 minutes. Remove chicken from skillet and drain on paper towels.

Discard all but 2 tablespoons (30 ml) of the frying oil. Over low heat, stir in 2 tablespoons (16 g) of the reserved flour mixture. Stirring constantly, cook for about 2 minutes. With a wire whisk, blend in beer and half-and-half. Stir in remaining 1 cup (235 ml) milk and bring to a boil over medium-high heat, stirring constantly. Reduce heat to low and simmer for about 5 minutes. Serve immediately with the chicken and mashed potatoes.

Prep = 15 minutes   **Cook** = 45 to 55 minutes   **Yield** = 4 servings

Turkey Hash Au Gratin with Porter and Potatoes

Making turkey hash from holiday leftovers is a great Sunday night dish. For a twist, substitute baked sweet potatoes for Idaho potatoes.

½ cup (112 g) of butter cut into tablespoons
1 cup (70 g) cremini mushrooms, sliced
1 shallot minced
½ cup (50 g) diced celery
1 clove crushed garlic
¼ cup (30 g) flour
1 teaspoon salt
¼ teaspoon black pepper
1 cup (235 ml) porter beer
1 cup (235 ml) half-and-half
¾ cup (180 g) heavy cream, beaten with 3 egg yolks
1 cup (120 g) grated Parmesan cheese
3 cups (525 g) cubed, cooked turkey
½ cup (70 g) drained, sliced pimentos
3 large baked potatoes, with skins on, cooled and cubed
¼ cup (28 g) breadcrumbs

In a medium, nonstick skillet, melt 3 tablespoons (42 g) of butter over medium heat. Sauté mushrooms, shallot, celery, and garlic for about 5 minutes, until tender. Set aside. In a large saucepan melt 4 tablespoons (56 g) of butter, and blend in flour, salt, and pepper. Cook stirring constantly until mixture bubbles. Blend in porter, half-and-half, and cream whisked with egg yolks. Cook, stirring constantly until sauce thickens and bubbles. Stir in ⅔ cup (80 g) of Parmesan cheese.

Combine turkey and potatoes in a large, buttered casserole dish. Pour sauce over the top. Melt remaining tablespoon of butter, and combine breadcrumbs with remaining cheese. Preheat oven to 350°F (180°C, or gas mark 4). Bake casserole for 25 to 30 minutes or until cheese topping is golden brown.

Prep = 20 minutes   **Cook** = 35 to 40 minutes   **Yield** = 6 servings

Stout-Glazed
Duck Breast

Red currant jam and red wine vinegar add
novel dimension to this beer-based sauce which is
reminiscent of a Cumberland. The secret is to reduce
the glaze until it is thick and syrupy.

4 boneless duck breasts (6 ounces, or 170 g, each)
1 teaspoon salt
4 shallots, minced
½ cup (120 ml) Guinness Stout
½ cup (150 g) seedless red currant jam
¼ cup (120 ml) red wine vinegar

Preheat oven to 350°F 180°C, or gas mark 4). Line a baking sheet
with aluminum foil. Make three slashes across the skin of each duck
breast at a 45-degree angle and sprinkle with salt. Heat a medium
nonstick skillet over high heat. When pan is hot, place duck breasts
in pan, skin side down, and cook for about 5 minutes, or until skin is
brown and crispy. Flip over and cook for 2 more minutes. Transfer
duck breasts, turned skin side up, to baking sheet.

Carefully remove all but 2 tablespoons (30 ml) of duck fat from
pan. Sauté shallots in pan until they begin to turn golden, about 3
minutes. Add Guinness and stir with a wooden spoon to loosen any
browned bits of duck. Add jam and vinegar, and boil for about 5
minutes, stirring occasionally. Meanwhile place baking sheet in oven
and cook duck for 6 minutes.

Remove from oven and slice each breast on the diagonal in
¼-inch (66 mm) strips. Arrange in a fanlike pattern on four warmed
plates. Spoon warm glaze over duck.

Prep = 10 minutes   **Cook** = 25 to 30 minutes   **Yield** = 4 servings

Hard Lemonade-Grilled Chicken

"Hard" lemonade (a.k.a. lemon-flavored malt beverage) is technically in the beer family. The asparagus are tossed on the grill during the last few minutes of cooking the chicken.

1 bottle (12 ounces, or 355 ml) hard lemonade, divided
¼ cup (60 ml) olive oil, plus extra for grill
1 clove garlic, crushed
6 boneless, skinless chicken breast halves
1 small onion, sliced
½ cup (112 g) mayonnaise
½ cup (115 g) sour cream
2 dozen fresh asparagus spears, washed and trimmed
Snipped fresh chives

Combine 1 cup (235 ml) of hard lemonade, olive oil, and garlic. Arrange chicken breasts in a casserole dish and cover with onions. Pour lemonade mixture over onions. Cover and refrigerate for 3 to 8 hours. Meanwhile, combine the remaining hard lemonade with mayonnaise and sour cream, blending until smooth.

Preheat grill to medium-high. Remove chicken from marinade, (discard marinade), and grill for about 7 minutes on each side. Lightly brush asparagus spears with olive oil and grill during the last 4 minutes of cooking the chicken. Arrange chicken on six plates, drizzle with sauce, and sprinkle with chives.

Prep = 15 minutes   **Chill** = 3 to 8 hours
Cook = 14 minutes   **Yield** = 6 servings

Henry's Balsamic-Beer Chicken

When Henry Schaffer, a friend in Connecticut, first served this dish to me, it appeared as though I was being served a platter of beef fillets. The balsamic vinegar gives the chicken breasts a deep rich, mahogany glaze. This recipe is both flavorful and heart healthy.

⅔ cup (156 ml) balsamic vinegar
⅓ cup (78 ml) beer
¼ cup (60 ml) olive oil
1 teaspoon salt
1 tablespoon (15 g) Dijon mustard
1 tablespoon (1.7 g) fresh rosemary, lightly chopped
1 teaspoon minced garlic
4 boneless, skinless chicken breasts
  (1 ½ to 2 pounds, or 680 to 905 g)
Nonstick cooking spray

In a large glass or ceramic bowl, combine vinegar, beer, olive oil, salt, mustard, rosemary, and garlic. Add chicken breasts. Cover and refrigerate for 24 hours, turning once.

Spray a large, nonstick skillet with nonstick cooking spray. Remove chicken from marinade and sauté in skillet over a medium-high heat for about 3 minutes on each, side to sear. Pour marinade over chicken. Cover and simmer for 10 minutes. Remove lid and continue to cook, to allow liquid to reduce, for about 5 minutes, or until sauce begins to thicken.

Prep = 10 minutes   **Chill** = 24 hours   **Cook** = 21 to 25 minutes
Yield = 4 servings

Henry's Heavy-on-the-Garlic Turkey Chili with Beer

Henry Schaffer makes his favorite chili with lots of fresh garlic, ground turkey, and beer. He likes to serve it over rice with Cheddar cheese corn bread. (Try the recipe on page 208).

1 tablespoon (15 ml) olive oil
1 large onion, chopped, divided
20 ounces (570 g) ground turkey
10 cloves garlic, chopped
4 tablespoons (30 g) chili powder
1 tablespoon (7 g) ground cumin
1 tablespoon (6 g) ground coriander
1 teaspoon (1.8 g) cayenne
2 teaspoons (12 g) salt
1 teaspoon pepper
2 cans (15 ounces, or 425 g, each) diced tomatoes, one drained, one undrained
1 can or bottle (12 ounces, or 355 ml) beer
1 can (15 ounces, or 425 g) red kidney beans
1 tablespoon (15 g) Frank's Red Hot Sauce
4 to 6 cups (660 to 990 g) steamed rice
1 cup (112 g) shredded Cheddar cheese

Heat olive oil in a large nonstick saucepan or stockpot. Reserve ⅓ cup (43 g) onion for later. Sauté the rest of onion in olive oil for 2 minutes. Add turkey and garlic, and sauté until turkey is browned. Add chili powder, cumin, coriander, cayenne, salt, pepper, tomatoes, beer, beans, and hot sauce. Bring to a boil, reduce heat, and simmer for 90 minutes.

Serve over rice, sprinkled with reserved onion and shredded cheese.

Prep = 15 minutes   **Cook** = 1 hour 45 minutes
Yield = 4 to 6 servings

India Pale Ale
British Chicken Curry

India pale ale is an amber beer brewed with pale
malts, with a strong hops flavor. As curries go, this is
the classic creamy version often associated
with many British recipes.

    1 stick (¼ pound, or 112 g) butter
    ½ cup (80 g) chopped onion
    ⅓ cup (50 g) seeded and diced red bell pepper
    ¼ cup (37 g) seeded and diced green bell pepper
3 to 5 teaspoons (6 to 10 g) curry powder
    ½ teaspoon salt
    ½ cup (63 g) all-purpose flour
    1 bottle (12 ounces, or 355 ml) India pale ale
    1 can (14 ounces, or 425 ml) condensed chicken broth
1 ½ cups (355 ml) heavy cream
    2 cups (220 g) cubed cooked chicken
    1 cup (165 g) golden raisins, packed
    Steamed rice
    Chutney
    Grated coconut
    Grape clusters

Melt butter in a large nonstick saucepan. Sauté onion and bell
peppers over medium heat until soft and tender. Blend in curry
powder and salt. Add flour and blend until absorbed into butter.
Gradually add beer, chicken broth, and cream. Cook, stirring constantly, until sauce thickens and boils. Stir in chicken and raisins.
Serve hot over steamed rice and garnish with chutney, coconut,
and clusters of grapes.

Prep = 25 minutes   **Cook** = 20 to 25 minutes   **Yield** = 4 servings

Jamaican Jerk Grilled Rock Cornish Game Hens

The Jamaican jerk seasoning is a blend of spices that can be purchased premixed or home-blended yourself.

- 1 cup Red Stripe beer or other lager
- 1 lemon, seeded and sliced
- 2 cloves garlic, crushed
- 2 tablespoons (30 ml) Worcestershire sauce
- ¼ cup (60 ml) peanut oil
- 2 tablespoons (28 g) Jamaican Jerk Seasoning, divided
- 4 Rock Cornish game hens
  skewers

Combine beer, lemon, garlic, Worcestershire sauce, peanut oil, and 1 tablespoon (14 g) of jerk seasoning in a glass measuring cup. Using poultry sheers, split game hens down the backbone and remove and discard the backbone. Snip wishbone and cut ½ inch (1.2 cm) into the backbone so that the bird can be pressed flat. Arrange game hens in a baking dish, pour marinade over top, cover with plastic wrap, and refrigerate for 4 hours. Remove from marinade and pat dry with paper towels, (discard marinade). Push a skewer horizontally through the wings and breast. Push another skewer horizontally through the wings and thighs. Rub skin with remaining tablespoon (14 g) of seasoning.

Heat grill to medium-high and grill game hens, cut side down, for 15 minutes. Turn skin side down and grill for an additional 10 minutes, or until the skin is crispy and there is no trace of pink at the bone. Remove skewers and serve.

JAMAICAN JERK SEASONING:
- ¼ cup (48 g) onion powder
- 2 tablespoons (5 g) dried chives
- 2 tablespoons (12 g) ground allspice
- 2 tablespoons (36 g) salt
- 2 tablespoons (30 g) dark brown sugar
- 1 tablespoon (6 g) black pepper
- 1 tablespoon (5 g) cayenne
- 1 tablespoon (9 g) garlic powder
- 1 teaspoon grated nutmeg
- 1 teaspoon ground cinnamon

Combine dry spices in an electric blender and process until chives are pulverized. Makes about 1 cup (192 g). Store in an airtight jar.

Prep = 25 minutes   **Chill** = 4 hours
Cook = 25 minutes   **Yield** = 4 servings

Lisa O'Brien's Beer-Poached Rosemary Chicken

My good friend and neighbor, Lisa O'Brien, developed a delicious method of oven-poaching chicken. It's not only simple but light and healthy. It's ideal for cooking chicken for chicken salad, as the meat takes on a lot of flavor.

6 boneless, skinless chicken breast halves
1 clove garlic, cut in half
3 tablespoons (45 ml) lemon juice
2 sprigs fresh rosemary, or 1 teaspoon dried
½ teaspoon salt
1 cup (235 ml) light lager

Preheat oven to 350°F (180°C, or gas mark 4). Place chicken breasts in an 8-inch (20 cm) square baking pan. Add garlic, lemon juice, and rosemary. Sprinkle with salt and cover with beer. Cover pan with aluminum foil and bake for 50 minutes.

Prep = 10 minutes   **Cook** = 50 minutes   **Yield** = 6 servings

Apple and Brown
Ale-Glazed Chicken

This recipe was inspired out of necessity.
How does one retrieve those pesky last spoonfuls
of steak sauce out of the bottle? Apple cider to the
rescue! Just pour it in and shake it up.
It's a good trick for extracting the
last drops from any narrow jar.

4 boneless, skinless chicken breast halves

1 tablespoon (14 g) butter

2 apples, cored and sliced but not peeled

1 tablespoon (15 ml) olive oil

½ cup (60 g) sliced red onion

½ cup (120 ml) apple cider

2 tablespoons (34 g) steak sauce

1 cup (235 ml) Newcastle Brown Ale

Slice chicken breasts into strips. In a large nonstick skillet, melt butter over medium heat and sauté apples until lightly browned. Set apples aside. Add olive oil to the pan, with onions and chicken. Sauté until chicken is lightly browned and onions are tender. Add apple cider, steak sauce, and beer. Continue cooking until sauce is reduced to a syrupy glaze, a little less than half of the original volume of liquid.

Prep = 15 minutes   **Cook** = 20 to 25 minutes   **Yield** = 4 servings

Oatmeal Stout-Maple-Mustard-Glazed Chicken

Maple syrup and oatmeal stout are a nice pairing for a grilled chicken. After a four-hour bath in beer, the chicken is ready to be barbecued on the grill with a stout-maple-mustard glaze.

1 chicken (3½ pounds, or 1.6 kg), cut up
Sprig of fresh rosemary
1 bottle (12 ounces, or 355 ml) oatmeal stout, divided
1 cup (235 g) maple syrup
⅓ cup (80 g) Dijon mustard
1 teaspoon seasoned salt
¼ teaspoon coarse ground black pepper
Olive oil, for grill

In a heavy-duty resealable plastic bag, place chicken pieces and rosemary. Pour 1 cup (235 ml) of stout over chicken and seal tightly. Allow to marinate in refrigerator for 4 hours. Add remaining ½ cup (120 ml) of stout to maple syrup and mustard. Bring to a boil and simmer for 4 minutes. Set aside half of glaze for a sauce and use the remaining half to baste while grilling.

Preheat grill to medium-high. Remove chicken from beer and blot dry with paper towels. Sprinkle with salt and pepper. Lightly coat grill with olive oil and place chicken pieces skin side up. Close grill hood and cook for 15 minutes. Turn chicken, cover, and cook for 20 to 40 minutes longer, turning occasionally and brushing several times with basting glaze, until juice of chicken is clear when thickest piece is cut to bone (170°F [77°C] for breasts; 180°F [82°C] for thighs and legs). Serve chicken with reserved glaze drizzled over the top.

Prep = 12 minutes   **Chill** = 4 hours
Cook = 40 minutes to 1 hour   **Yield** = 4 servings

Pale Ale Chicken
Paprikash

When I came across this Hungarian chicken recipe, I was tempted to substitute chicken breasts for thighs. However, the thigh meat actually adds a more authentic character to the dish.

1 cup (125 g) all-purpose flour

2 ½ teaspoons (6 g) paprika

¼ teaspoon cayenne

¼ teaspoon ground ginger

1 teaspoon basil, chopped

⅛ teaspoon grated nutmeg

1 teaspoon salt

¼ teaspoon freshly ground pepper

12 chicken thighs, skinned and boned

4 tablespoons (55 g) butter

1 large clove garlic, finely minced

1 bottle (12 ounces, or 355 ml) pale ale beer

1 can (13 ounces, or 369 ml) condensed chicken broth

2 cups (460 g) sour cream

2 tablespoons (30 ml) Worcestershire sauce

Preheat oven to 325°F (170°C, or gas mark 3). In a large resealable plastic bag, combine flour, paprika, cayenne, ginger, basil, nutmeg, salt, and pepper. Shake chicken pieces, a few at a time, in flour mixture. Melt butter in a large nonstick skillet, brown chicken on all sides, and transfer to a baking dish. Sauté garlic in drippings for 2 minutes. Stir in beer, chicken broth, sour cream, and Worcestershire sauce. Heat through, stirring constantly, but do not boil. Pour over chicken. Bake, uncovered, for 1 hour, or until chicken is tender.

Prep = 20 minutes   **Cook** = 1 hour 15 minutes
Yield = 6 servings

Seafood

Pecan-Crusted Trout
with Porter Glaze

Almost any porter will bring out the rich,
nutty flavor of toasted pecans. Always watch pecans
like a hawk when roasting them in the oven,
as they can go from toasty to burned in the
blink of an eye.

4 large trout fillets
Juice of 1 lemon
Salt and pepper
½ cup (57 g) seasoned dried bread crumbs, divided
2 teaspoons (2.5 g) rosemary
1 cup (100 g) toasted pecans
1 egg beaten with 1 tablespoon (15 ml) water
⅓ cup (42 g) all-purpose flour
2 tablespoons (30 ml) vegetable oil, divided
2 tablespoons (28 g) butter, divided
1 cup (235 g) porter

Coat trout fillets with lemon juice and sprinkle lightly with salt and
pepper. Allow to stand for about 10 minutes. Combine ¼ cup (27 g)
of bread crumbs with pecans and coarsely grind in food processor.
Combine with remaining bread crumbs in a shallow dish. Put egg
wash in a shallow bowl. Dredge trout fillets with flour and dip in
egg wash. Place skin side up in pecan-crumb mixture, pressing
pecan mixture into flesh.

Cook two fillets at a time: In large nonstick skillet, melt 1 tablespoon (15 ml/14g) each of oil and butter. Place fillets skin side up in
skillet with coating facing down. Cook until golden brown, 3 to 4
minutes. Using spatula, carefully turn fillets skin side down. Cook for
3 minutes, until opaque. Transfer trout to a warm platter and repeat
with remaining two fillets, oil, and butter. Deglaze pan with porter
and reduce until syrupy. Drizzle over trout fillets.

To toast pecans: Preheat oven to 350°F (180°C, or gas mark 4) and
spread pecans on a baking sheet. Bake for 5 to 8 minutes, stirring
once or twice, until evenly golden brown. Watch carefully to avoid
burning.

Prep = 20 minutes   **Cook** = 30 minutes   **Yield** = 4 servings

Bayou Catfish
in Beer-Batter
and Remoulade

When I was a kid, I could catch a catfish anywhere
I seemed to throw in a fishing line, whether it was at
a lake or on the beach. It wasn't until I was
much older that I discovered what a
delicacy it could be.

REMOULADE SAUCE:
- 1 cup (225 g) mayonnaise
- 3 tablespoons (45 g) Creole mustard
- 2 tablespoons (35 g) chili sauce
- 2 tablespoons (20 g) chopped bread-and-butter pickles
- 2 tablespoons (8 g) chopped fresh parsley

BEER BATTER:
- 1 cup (235 ml) beer
- 2 eggs
- ½ teaspoon salt
- ¼ cup (35 g) cornmeal
- 1 teaspoon paprika
- 1 teaspoon baking powder
- 1 teaspoon garlic powder
- 1 cup (125 g) all-purpose flour

- 6 boned catfish fillets
- Oil, for frying

For remoulade sauce: Combine remoulade ingredients in small bowl
until blended and chill until serving.

For beer batter: In a bowl, combine beer, eggs, salt, cornmeal, paprika, baking powder, garlic powder, and flour. Allow to stand for about
30 minutes.
   Preheat oil in a deep fryer to 375°F (190°C). Dip catfish fillets in
batter, one at a time, and fry in oil until golden brown on both sides,
turning once. Catfish fillets can be cut in half if they are too large to
handle. Serve with remoulade sauce.

Prep = 20 minutes **Stand** = 30 minutes
Cook = 35 minutes **Yield** = 6 servings

Tyler's Soft Fish Tacos

Tyler Taylor is a friend, interior designer, and fish taco fan. With her version, the fish is dipped in beer batter, fried, and rolled in soft flour tortillas.

1 pound cod, halibut, or mahi mahi cut into 1-inch (2.5 cm) strips
1 cup plus 1 tablespoon (133 g) all-purpose flour, divided
½ teaspoon salt
1 teaspoon black pepper
¼ teaspoon cayenne
1 teaspoon hot pepper sauce
1 teaspoon black pepper
1 cup (235 ml) flat beer
Juice of ½ lime
Vegetable oil, for frying
Soft flour tortillas
Guacamole
Salsa
Shredded lettuce

Pat fish dry and dredge lightly with 1 tablespoon (8 g) of flour. Combine remaining flour with salt, black pepper, cayenne, hot sauce, pepper, beer, and lime juice. Whisk until smooth. Preheat an electric fryer filled with oil to 375°F (190°C). Dip fish pieces in batter, and fry until crisp and golden brown. Drain well on paper towels. Serve fish rolled in flour tortillas with guacamole, salsa, and shredded lettuce.

Prep = 25 minutes   **Cook** = 12 minutes   **Yield** = 6 servings

Tyler's Mussels in Guinness and Garlic

Tyler Taylor created this simple, yet elegant, dish. If you enjoy mussels steamed in wine, you'll truly appreciate the unique flavor that a dark beer can add. Remember to discard any mussels that don't open after cooking.

4 pounds (2 kg) mussels
24 ounces (720 ml) Guinness Stout
2 cloves crushed garlic
Salt and black pepper
2 tablespoons (6 g) fresh chives, minced
Juice of one lime
8 tablespoons (1 stick or 112 g) butter, melted

Wash mussels, scrubbing under running water. Discard any that are broken or slightly open. Place mussels in a large stockpot. Combine beer with garlic and chives, and pour over mussels. Sprinkle with salt and pepper. Cover with lid and bring to a boil for about 8 to 10 minutes. Serve with lime wedges and melted butter.

Prep = 15 minutes   **Cook** = 14 to 16 minutes   **Yield** = 4 Servings

Baja Scallops
in Beer Batter

Cornmeal adds texture and character to
beer-battered seafood. The sauce also works well with
Tyler's Soft Fish Tacos (see page 140).

BAJA SAUCE:
- ½ cup (115 g) plain yogurt
- ½ cup (112 g) mayonnaise
- Juice of 1 lime
- 1 jalapeño, minced
- 1 teaspoon minced capers
- ½ teaspoon dried oregano
- ½ teaspoon ground cumin
- ½ teaspoon dried dill
- 1 teaspoon cayenne

BEER-BATTERED SCALLOPS:
- 1 cup plus 2 tablespoons (138 g) all-purpose flour, divided
- 3 tablespoons (27 g) cornmeal
- 1 egg, beaten
- ½ teaspoon salt
- ½ teaspoon pepper
- 1 teaspoon garlic powder
- ¼ teaspoon cayenne
- 1 can (12 ounces, or 355 ml) beer
- 2 pounds (905 g) scallops, cut into ¾-inch (1.8 cm) pieces if large
- Vegetable oil, for frying

For Baja sauce: Combine yogurt, mayonnaise, lime, jalapeño, capers, oregano, cumin, dill, and cayenne in a medium bowl with wire whisk until smooth. Keep chilled until serving time.

For beer-battered scallops: Mix 1 cup (110 g) of flour, cornmeal, egg, salt, pepper, garlic powder, and cayenne in medium bowl. Add enough beer, blending thoroughly, to get the consistency of a thick pancake batter.

Preheat a deep fryer filled with oil to 375°F (190°C). Pat scallops dry and dredge in 2 tablespoons (28 g) of flour. Dip in beer batter and fry a few pieces at a time until golden brown and crispy. Serve with Baja sauce for dipping.

Prep = 20 minutes   **Cook** = 30 minutes   **Yield** = 6 servings

Beer-Baked Cod
Amandine

If you are in a hurry, this dish is a no-fuss way
to prepare fresh fish. Orange roughy and perch
can be used interchangeably with cod.

8 tablespoons (1 stick or 112 g) butter, melted, divided
6 ounces (half of a 12-ounce [355-ml] can) flat beer, divided
3 tablespoons (45 ml) lemon juice
6 cod fillets (6 ounces, or 170 g, each)
½ cup (62 g) sliced almonds

Preheat oven to 325°F (170°C, or gas mark 3). Combine 3 tablespoons (42 g) of butter with 3 tablespoons (45 ml) of beer and
lemon juice. Coat a 9 × 13-inch (22.5 × 32.5 cm) glass baking dish
with the remaining butter. Arrange cod in dish and baste with half
of lemon-butter mixture. Sprinkle with almonds. Bake, basting with
remaining lemon-butter mixture, just until fish flakes easily and
almonds begin to brown.

Prep = 5 minutes   **Cook** = 10 minutes   **Yield** = 6 servings

Beer-Broiled Shrimp

Many recipes call for beer-boiled shrimp, but this one marinates the shrimp in beer then broils it. These are so flavorful, they hardly need a dipping sauce.

1 cup (235 ml) beer
¼ cup (60 ml) olive oil
2 tablespoons (4 g) chopped fresh parsley
1 tablespoon (4 g) snipped fresh chives
4 teaspoons (23 ml) Worcestershire sauce
1 clove garlic, crushed
½ teaspoon salt
⅛ teaspoon pepper
2 pounds (905 g) large shrimp, shelled and deveined

In a large glass bowl, combine beer, olive oil, parsley, chives, Worcestershire sauce, garlic, salt, and pepper. Add shrimp and stir. Cover and let stand at room temperature for 1 hour. Drain, reserving marinade.

Place shrimp on oiled broiler rack and broil 4 to 5 inches (10.2 to 12.7 cm) from heat for 4 minutes. Turn and brush with marinade. Broil for 2 to 4 minutes more, or until light pink.

Prep = 10 minutes   **Stand** = 1 hour   **Cook** = 6 to 8 minutes
Yield = 4 servings

British Beer-Battered Fish and Chips

Try a brown ale for this traditional fish-and-chips recipe. The nutty brown color adds character to the batter. Be prepared to keep the potatoes warm in the oven while frying the fish.

1 ½ cups (185 g) all-purpose flour
1 cup (235 ml) flat beer
4 teaspoons (20 ml) vegetable oil, plus extra for frying
½ teaspoon Old Bay Seasoning
½ teaspoon paprika
1 egg, separated
4 medium russet potatoes, each cut into 8 wedges
1 pound (455 g) cod fillets (cut each fillet in half and pat dry)
Salt
Vegetable oil, for frying
Malt vinegar, for serving
Lemon wedges, for serving

In a small bowl, combine flour, beer, 4 teaspoons (20 ml) oil, Old Bay Seasoning, and paprika. Cover and refrigerate for 1 to 2 hours. Blend egg yolk into batter. Beat egg white in separate bowl until soft peaks form. Gently fold into batter.

Preheat oven to 200°F (93°C, or gas mark ¼) and line a baking sheet with a paper towel. Preheat oil in a deep fryer to 365°F (185°C). Keep an extra stack of paper towels on hand for draining fish and potatoes.

Fry potato wedges in small batches for 4 to 6 minutes, until golden brown. Drain on paper towels and sprinkle with salt. Allow temperature to return to 365°F (185°C) between batches. Keep fried potatoes warm in oven while frying fish.

Dust fish lightly with cornstarch and dip about four pieces at a time in batter. Fry for 4 to 6 minutes, or until golden brown and crisp. Drain on paper towels. Allow oil to return to 365°F (185°C) between batches. Serve fish with potatoes, malt vinegar, and lemon wedges.

Prep = 20 minutes   **Chill** = 1 to 2 hours   **Cook** = 35 minutes
Yield = 4 servings

Classic Beer-Battered Shrimp with Mustard-Fruit Marmalade

The spicy orange marmalade dip is a signature of this retro dish. There are many versions of the batter but using one without eggs makes it crispier and less doughnutlike in texture.

1 cup (125 g) all-purpose flour, plus extra for dredging
1 tablespoon (7 g) paprika
1 tablespoon (18 g) salt
1 can (12 ounces, or 355 ml) beer
16 jumbo shrimp
   Vegetable oil, for frying

MUSTARD-FRUIT MARMALADE:
   1 cup (320 g) orange marmalade
   ¼ cup (66 ml) lemon juice
   2 tablespoons (35 g) frozen orange juice concentrate, thawed
   2 tablespoons (30 g) horseradish
   ½ teaspoon ground ginger
   ½ teaspoon salt
   ½ teaspoon dry mustard

Combine 1 cup (125 g) of flour, paprika, and salt in a medium bowl. Blend in beer with a wire whisk until smooth. Chill batter at least 1 hour. Preheat oil to 375°F (190°C) in a deep fryer. Dredge shrimp in flour, dip in batter, and deep-fry until golden brown. Fry shrimp a few at a time, taking care not to crowd them. Serve with mustard-fruit marmalade.

For Mustard-Fruit Marmalade: Combine ingredients in blender and blend until smooth.

Prep = 20 minutes   **Chill** = 1 hour   **Cook** = 20 minutes
Yield = 4 to 8 servings

Crab Cakes with Beer-Reduction Remoulade

Beer and crab cakes are such a great pairing that it seems only natural to serve them with a beer-flavored remoulade.

1 pound (455 g) fresh crabmeat
1 teaspoon Old Bay Seasoning
¼ teaspoon dry mustard
1 tablespoon (15 g) mayonnaise
1 tablespoon (15 ml) Worcestershire sauce
¼ teaspoon salt
1 tablespoon (4 g) chopped fresh parsley
1 egg, beaten
½ cup (57 g) dried bread crumbs
  Vegetable oil, for frying
  Lemon wedges, for serving

BEER-REDUCTION REMOULADE:
1 tablespoon (15 ml) olive oil
2 cloves garlic, crushed
1 shallot, minced
1 cup (235 ml) beer
1 teaspoon Worcestershire sauce
1 cup (225 g) mayonnaise
2 tablespoons (20 g) chopped bread-and-butter pickles
  Pinch of cayenne
  Salt and pepper

In a medium bowl, combine crabmeat, Old Bay Seasoning, dry mustard, mayonnaise, Worcestershire sauce, salt, parsley, egg, and bread crumbs, using your hands or a rubber spatula.

Shape into small rounds, flatten slightly with metal spatula, Heat about ½ inch (1.2 cm) of oil in a skillet and brown cakes on both sides. Serve warm with lemon wedges and remoulade.

For remoulade: In a small nonstick saucepan over medium heat, heat olive oil and sauté garlic and shallot for about 3 minutes. Add beer and simmer until mixture reduced to about ¼ cup (60 ml).

Remove from heat and cool. Blend in mayonnaise, Worcestershire sauce, pickles, and cayenne. Season with salt and pepper to taste.

Prep = 20 minutes   **Cook** = 20 minutes   **Yield** = 4 servings

Soft-Shell Crabs in Butter and Beer

Small soft-shell crabs, or "busters" as they are referred to along the Gulf Coast, are a delicacy. They are a real treat for a candlelit dinner for two or an appetizer for four. For an interesting twist, try deglazing the pan with a lambic beer. The acidity complements most seafood.

- 8 tablespoons (1 stick or 112 g) butter, divided
- ½ cup (62 g) sliced, blanched almonds
- 4 small soft-shell crabs, dressed
- All-purpose flour, for dredging
- 1 tablespoon (45 ml) lemon juice
- ½ cup (120 ml) beer
- 1 tablespoon (4 g) minced fresh parsley
- 1 tablespoon (4 g) snipped fresh chives
- Lemon wedges, for serving

Melt 1 tablespoon (14 g) of butter in a small skillet and sauté almonds, stirring constantly, until golden brown, then set aside. Meanwhile, dredge crabs lightly with flour and shake off excess. Heat remaining butter in a medium nonstick skillet. Once it is hot and foaming, add crabs. Sauté over high heat, turning occasionally with tongs, until crisp and reddish-brown, about 5 minutes. Transfer crabs to a heated platter. Add lemon juice and beer to the skillet and bring to a boil. Stir in parsley and chives, then pour over crabs. Top with almonds, and serve with lemon wedges.

Prep = 15 minutes **Cook** = 12 minutes **Yield** = 2 servings

Dilled Grilled Swordfish Skewers in White Ale

Belgian white ale is a great pairing with seafood dishes and brings out the flavor of dill and cucumbers. This recipe can also be prepared with salmon or halibut.

- 2 pounds (905 g) fresh swordfish steaks, cut 1-inch (2.5 cm) thick
- 1 cup (235 ml) Blue Moon or Belgium white ale
- ¼ cup (60 ml) lemon juice
- ⅓ cup (78 ml) olive oil
- 1 bay leaf
- 1 tablespoon (2 g) snipped fresh dill
- ¼ teaspoon coarsely ground black pepper
- 1 large cucumber, halved lengthwise and cut into ¾-inch (1.8 cm) thick slices
- 6 ounces (half of a 12-ounce [340 g] jar) roasted red peppers, drained and sliced into 1-inch (2.5 cm) pieces
- 12 small to medium mushrooms or baby bella mushrooms

Rinse swordfish; pat dry with paper towels. If necessary, remove bones and skin. Cut into 1-inch (2.5 cm) cubes. Place swordfish cubes in resealable plastic bag set into shallow dish. For marinade, in small bowl, combine beer, lemon juice, olive oil, bay leaf, dill, and black pepper. Pour over swordfish and seal bag. Marinate at room temperature for 30 minutes, turning bag occasionally. Drain fish, reserving marinade. On six long metal skewers, alternately thread fish, cucumber, red peppers, and mushrooms.

Brush with marinade. Preheat grill to medium and place kebabs on a greased rack. Cook for 8 to 12 minutes, or until fish flakes easily when tested with a fork, turning and brushing with reserved marinade halfway through grilling time. Discard any remaining marinade.

Prep = 15 minutes   **Marinate** = 30 minutes
Cook = 8 to 12 minutes   **Yield** = 6 servings

Stout Grilled Tuna Teriyaki Steaks with Orange Aioli

Aioli is a garlicky, mayonnaise-type sauce
that is nicely accented with orange flavor for seafood.

TERIYAKI MARINADE:

¼ cup (85 g) honey, warmed

¼ cup (60 ml) light soy sauce, or 3 tablespoons (42 ml)
tamari sauce

3 tablespoons (52 g) frozen orange juice concentrate, thawed

⅓ cup (78 ml) Guinness Stout

3 tablespoons (45 ml) olive or other vegetable oil,
plus extra for grilling

2 tablespoons (30 g) brown sugar, firmly packed

1 tablespoon (15 ml) dark sesame oil

⅛ teaspoon ground ginger, or ½ teaspoon chopped fresh ginger
Freshly ground black pepper

6 tuna steaks (about 2 pounds, or 905 g)

ORANGE AIOLI:

1 head garlic

Olive oil

1 cup (225 g)mayonnaise

2 tablespoons (35 g) orange juice concentrate, thawed

2 tablespoons (30 ml) Guinness Stout

Blend the marinade ingredients in a bowl and let stand at room
temperature for 1 hour. Brush marinade over fish and refrigerate for
1 hour before grilling.

Preheat grill to medium-high and brush rack with a little additional olive oil. Grill tuna steaks for 5 minutes on each side, or until it
flakes easily with a fork. Serve topped with orange aioli.

For aioli: Preheat oven to 300°F (150°C, or gas mark 2). Brush garlic
cloves with oil and roast garlic head until completely soft. Squeeze
cloves from skins and mash. Blend with mayonnaise, orange juice,
and Guinness.

Prep = 25 minutes　**Stand/Chill** = 2 hours　**Cook** = 10 minutes
Yield = 6 servings

Pilsner-Poached
Salmon with Dill

Poaching seafood is about the simplest and
healthiest way to prepare it. Typically wine or stock
is used, but beer is an excellent alternative. For a
richer dish, serve with dill hollandaise sauce.

2 cups (475 ml) pilsner
½ small onion
1 bunch fresh dill, tied with kitchen string
4 salmon fillets (4 ounces, or 115 g, each)

DILL HOLLANDAISE SAUCE:
3 egg yolks
Juice of ½ lemon
1 teaspoon cold water
1 teaspoon salt
1 teaspoon snipped fresh dill
1 teaspoon ground black pepper
½ cup (112 g) soft butter

In a skillet with a cover, bring pilsner, onion, and dill to a boil. Reduce
to a simmer over low heat and place salmon fillets in beer mixture.
Cover and poach for 15 minutes, or until fish flakes easily with a
fork. Serve with dill hollandaise sauce.

For dill hollandaise sauce: In the top of a double boiler over
simmering water, whisk together egg yolks, lemon juice, cold water,
salt, dill, and pepper. Gradually whisk butter into yolk mixture while
cooking over simmering water. Continue whisking over low heat for
8 minutes, or until sauce is thickened. Serve immediately. If sauce
breaks down, re-emulsify with a few drops of lemon juice or cold
water.

Prep = 10 minutes   **Cook** = 18 minutes
Yield = 4 servings

Kirin-Glazed Salmon

Ginger-laced Kirin-glazed salmon has become a popular restaurant dish. The Japanese beer Kirin is used in this recipe; however, almost any Asian beer will work well.

- 2 tablespoons (16 g) grated ginger
- 2 tablespoons (20 g) minced garlic
- 2 tablespoons (12 g) scallions, sliced thinly (white part only, reserve green stems for garnish)
- 2 tablespoons (2 g) chopped cilantro
- 1 tablespoon (14 g) hot chili paste
- ⅓ cup (78 ml) white rice vinegar
- ¾ cup (175 ml) Kirin or other Asian beer
- 2 tablespoons (62 g) hoisin sauce
- 1 tablespoon (15 g) dark brown sugar
- 2 teaspoons (10 ml) sesame oil, divided
- 2 tablespoons (28 ml) peanut oil
- 4 salmon steaks

In a small saucepan, combine ginger, garlic, scallion, cilantro, chili paste, rice vinegar, beer, hoisin sauce, brown sugar, and 1 teaspoon of sesame oil. Bring to a boil and reduce to about half, or until syrupy.

Preheat oven to 450°F (230°C, or gas mark 8). In a heavy-bottomed ovenproof skillet on a stovetop burner, combine peanut oil and remaining sesame oil and sear salmon on one side. Turn salmon over in pan. Remove from heat and baste with glaze. Roast in oven for another 3 minutes. Serve brushed with remaining glaze and garnish with a sprinkling of sliced green scallions.

Prep = 20 minutes   **Cook** = 18 to 25 minutes   **Yield** = 4 servings

Beerbecue

Apple Butter
Beerbecue Sauce

This sauce is based on an heirloom recipe
dating back to a family apple orchard in Saint
Joseph, Missouri. Back then, apple wood was used to
smoke meats—a method that is popular again today.
The mild flavor of apple butter is a perfect addition
to barbecue sauce for pork ribs or chicken.

1 tablespoon (14 g) butter
1 tablespoon (15 ml) olive oil
½ cup (80 g) finely chopped onion
¼ cup (30 g) finely chopped celery
2 cups (480 g) ketchup
1 cup (282 g) apple butter
1 bottle (12 ounces, or 355 ml) apple ale
¼ cup (60 ml) cider vinegar
½ cup (112 g) dark brown sugar, firmly packed
½ teaspoon dry mustard
1 tablespoon (15 ml) Worcestershire sauce
1 teaspoon (5 ml) hickory smoke flavor

Melt butter and olive oil in a large nonstick skillet and sauté onion
and celery until tender. Add ketchup, apple butter, ale, vinegar,
brown sugar, mustard, Worcestershire sauce, and smoke flavor.
Bring to a boil, then simmer, uncovered, until sauce is reduced
by about one-third in volume.

Prep = 10 minutes   **Cook** = 20 to 30 minutes
Yield = About 3 cups (235 ml)

Beerbecue
Baked Beans

Ever been to a potluck where the obligatory
baked beans seemed to be in every casserole on the
table? Next time that happens, remember that
simmering beans in beer helps them
stand out from the crowd.

          4 strips uncooked bacon
          1 cup (150 g) seeded and chopped green bell pepper
          1 cup (160 g) chopped red onion
          1 can (32 ounces, or 905 g) pork and beans
          1 cup (240 g) ketchup
      1 ½ cups (355 ml) flat beer
          1 cup (225 g) brown sugar, firmly packed

In a large nonstick saucepan, cook bacon until crisp. Remove strips
from pan and set aside on paper towels to drain. Add bell pepper
and onions to bacon fat and sauté until onions are transparent.

   Stir in pork and beans, ketchup, beer, and brown sugar. Simmer
over low heat for 15 to 20 minutes, or until slightly thickened.

Preheat oven to 350°F (180°C, or gas mark 4) and grease a 3-quart
(1.5 L) casserole. Pour bean mixture into casserole and bake for 50
to 60 minutes.

Prep = 10 minutes   **Cook** = 1 hour 5 minutes to 1 hour 20 minutes
Yield = 8 to 10 servings

Buttery Beerbecue Sauce

Aside from the usual ribs and chicken, this is one of those barbecue sauces that just seems right at home on a steak. Be sure to use real butter, not margarine, as it is essential for the correct flavor.

- ½ cup (112 g) butter
- 1 medium onion, finely chopped
- 1 clove garlic, crushed
- 1 bottle (12 ounces, or 355 ml) beer
- 1 tablespoon (15 g) brown sugar
- 1 teaspoon salt
- ½ teaspoon black pepper
- ½ teaspoon chili powder
- 4 drops hot pepper sauce
- 2 tablespoons (30 ml) Worcestershire sauce
- ¼ cup (60 g) ketchup

In a medium saucepan, melt butter over low heat. Add onion and garlic, and cook until soft but not brown. Add beer, brown sugar, salt, pepper, chili powder, hot pepper sauce, Worcestershire sauce, and ketchup. Bring to a boil, reduce heat, and simmer, uncovered, for 15 minutes.

Prep = 10 minutes   **Cook** = 25 minutes   **Yield** = 1 ¼ cups (285 ml)

Backward Beerbecued Ribs with Bourbon

What makes this recipe unique is that it goes on the grill first and then into the oven. The ribs are braised in the sauce until they are tender but not falling off the bone.

6 pounds (2.7 kg) pork baby back ribs
Sea salt
½ cup (120 ml) Jack Daniels or other bourbon whiskey

BEER AND MOLASSES BARBECUE SAUCE:
1 bottle (12 ounces, or 340 g) chili sauce
1 ¼ cups (425 g) molasses
1 bottle (12 ounces, or 355 ml) beer
1 tablespoon (15 ml) soy sauce
2 tablespoons (15 g) chili powder
2 tablespoons (30 ml) lime juice
2 teaspoons (10 ml) liquid smoke

Remove the back sinew of the ribs. Preheat grill to medium-high. Lightly sprinkle ribs with salt. Sear both sides of ribs on hot grill, until there are obvious char marks.

For barbecue sauce: Combine chili sauce, molasses, beer, soy sauce, chili powder, lime juice, and liquid smoke in a large saucepan. Bring to a boil and simmer until reduced by one-third of the original volume.

Preheat oven to 350°F (180°C, or gas mark 4). Place chargrilled ribs in a nonstick roasting pan (or spray pan with nonstick cooking spray). Combine the bourbon and barbecue sauce, and pour over the ribs. Cover with foil and braise in oven until tender but not falling of the bone, between 1 and 1 ½ hours.

Prep = 20 minutes   **Cook** = 1 ½ to 2 hours   **Yield** = 6 servings

Carolina-Style
Beerbecued Chicken

South Carolina is known for its tomato-free vinegar-based barbecue sauces that really bring a sweat to the brow. This version is great for chicken.

- 1 fryer chicken (3 pounds, or 1.4 kg), cut up
- ¾ cup (175 ml) beer
- 1 ¼ cups (285 ml) cider vinegar
- 1 teaspoon dry mustard
- 5 tablespoons (38 g) chili powder
- 1 teaspoon paprika
- ¼ cup (50 g) sugar
- 1 teaspoon black pepper
- 1 teaspoon cayenne
- ½ teaspoon ground cumin

Arrange chicken pieces in a glass baking dish. Blend together beer, cider vinegar, mustard, chili powder, paprika, sugar, black pepper, cayenne, and cumin. Spoon ¼ cup (60 ml) sauce over chicken, set aside another ¼ cup (60 ml) sauce for basting, and separately reserve the remaining sauce to serve with the cooked chicken (do not use for basting). Let chicken stand 20 minutes, turning once. Preheat grill to medium. Cook chicken pieces over grill for 30 minutes, or until juices run clear, turning occasionally and basting with the ¼ cup (60 ml) of sauce. Serve chicken with reserved sauce.

Prep = 10 minutes   **Stand** = 20 minutes
Cook = 30 minutes   **Yield** = 4 servings

Carolina White Beerbecue Sauce

It's odd calling a mayonnaise-based recipe a barbecue sauce. Surprisingly, it gives a nice glaze to poultry and meats when used as a basting sauce while grilling. It also serves as a nice condiment for meats and sandwiches. Any beer can be used, but an apple ale flavors this nicely.

1 cup (225 g) mayonnaise
⅓ cup (66 g) sugar
½ teaspoon salt
½ teaspoon dry mustard
½ teaspoon onion powder
½ teaspoon garlic powder
½ teaspoon ground black pepper
⅔ cup (156 ml) cider vinegar
⅔ cup (156 ml) apple ale or pale-colored beer

In a small bowl, blend sugar, salt, dry mustard, onion powder, garlic powder and black pepper into mayonnaise, using a wire whisk. Slowly blend in vinegar and beer to smooth out any lumps. Use as a grilling sauce or condiment on smoked meats.

Prep = 8 minutes   **Cook** = N/A
Yield = About 2 ⅓ cups (553 ml)

Chili-Lime Mesquite Beerbecue Sauce

This is an excellent sauce for brisket or beef short ribs. I will even serve it on top of meat loaf. Whether you are oven-baking in the middle of January or grilling outdoors in June, this is a must-have sauce to keep on hand.

- 2 tablespoons (30 ml) olive oil
- 2 cloves garlic, crushed
- 1 cup (160 ml) finely chopped onions
- 1 cup (150 ml) seeded and finely chopped bell peppers
- ½ cup (142 g) frozen limeade concentrate
- 2 tablespoons (15 g) chili powder
- 1 teaspoon instant coffee granules
- ½ teaspoon salt
- 1 tablespoon (11 g) mustard seeds
- 1 can (15 ounces, or 425 g) tomato sauce
- 2 bottles (12 ounces, or 340 g, each) chili sauce
- 1 can (12 ounces, or 355 ml) beer
- 1 tablespoon (15 ml) mesquite smoke flavoring

Heat olive oil in a large nonstick saucepan. Sauté garlic, onions, and bell peppers until tender. Stir in lime juice concentrate, chili powder, coffee, salt, mustard seeds, tomato sauce, chili sauce, beer, and mesquite smoke. Bring to a boil. Reduce heat and simmer, uncovered, until sauce is about the consistency of ketchup.

Prep = 15 minutes   **Cook** = 30 to 35 minutes
Yield = 1 quart (946 ml)

Chuck Wagon Beerbecue Roll

This sandwich is a regional variation of the popular pulled pork. Often referred to as "Pit BBQ," it can easily be replicated in a slow cooker.

- 3 pounds (1.4 kg) beef chuck, cut into cubes
- 2 cups (320 g) chopped onions
- 3 small green bell peppers, seeded and chopped
- 1 can (6 ounces, or 170 g) tomato paste
- ½ cup (120 g) brown sugar, packed
- ¼ cup (60 ml) cider vinegar
- ¼ cup 30 g) chili powder
- 2 teaspoons (12 g) salt
- 1 teaspoon dry mustard
- 2 teaspoons (10 ml) Worcestershire sauce
- 2 tablespoons (30 ml) liquid smoke
- 1 cup (235 ml) beer
- 8 toasted sandwich buns

Combine beef, onions, bell peppers, tomato paste, brown sugar, vinegar, chili powder, salt, dry mustard, Worcestershire sauce, liquid smoke, and beer in a slow cooker. Cover and cook on high setting for 6 to 8 hours, or until meat is starting to fall apart. Shred meat with a fork and serve warm on toasted buns.

Prep = 10 minutes   **Cook** = 6 to 8 hours   **Yield** = 8 servings

Irish Whiskey Beerbecue Sauce

This is the Celtic version of Jack Daniels barbecue sauce. It can also be made with a porter. It a simple sauce to make that's great on ribs, burgers, or steaks.

- 2 cups (480 g) ketchup
- 1 cup (225 g) dark brown sugar, packed
- 3 tablespoons (45 ml) Worcestershire sauce
- 2 teaspoons (6 g) dry mustard
- ½ cup (120 ml) Irish whiskey
- ½ cup (120 ml) Guinness Extra Stout
- 4 tablespoons (60 ml) cider vinegar
- 4 tablespoons (60 ml) soy sauce
- ½ teaspoon cayenne
- ½ teaspoon liquid smoke (optional)

Combine all ingredients in 2-quart (1 L) saucepan. Bring to a boil over high heat, stirring occasionally. Reduce heat to low and simmer, uncovered, for 20 minutes, stirring occasionally, until sauce is slightly reduced and thickened.

Prep = 8 minutes   **Cook** = 25 minutes
Yield = About 2 ½ cups (595 ml)

Maple-Bacon
Beerbecue Sauce

This Vermont-inspired sauce is great for basting
beef kebabs or steaks on the grill. Be sure to use
hickory-smoked bacon or else add a teaspoon
of hickory smoke flavor to the sauce.

   6 strips uncooked hickory-smoked bacon,
      cut into matchstick pieces
   1 cup (160 g) chopped onion
1 ½ cups (360 g) ketchup
   ½ cup (120 ml) cider vinegar
   1 bottle (12 ounces, or 355 ml) oatmeal stout
   1 cup (235 g) maple syrup
   2 tablespoons (30 ml) Worcestershire sauce
   ½ teaspoon coarsely ground black pepper

In a large nonstick saucepan, sauté bacon until it begins to crisp
and fat is rendered. Add onions and sauté until tender. Add ketchup,
vinegar, stout, maple syrup, Worcestershire sauce, and black pepper,
and bring to a boil. Reduce heat to low and simmer, uncovered, until
thickened to a syrupy consistency, 30 to 40 minutes.

Prep = 10 minutes   **Cook** = 35 to 45 minutes
Yield = About 3 cups (710 ml)

Slow-Cooker Honey Beerbecue Sauce

Any stout will work well with this recipe,
but the combination of oatmeal with honey is
particularly flavorful. This one needs to simmer
a long time; try using a slow cooker
to streamline the process.

1 cup (150 g) seeded and chopped green bell pepper
3 cups (480 g) chopped onion
½ cup (170 g) honey
3 cloves garlic, crushed
2 tablespoons (30 ml) lemon juice
2 teaspoons (12 g) salt
2 tablespoons (30 ml) Worcestershire sauce
1 bottle (12 ounces, or 355 ml) oatmeal stout
3 tablespoons (45 ml) vinegar
2 teaspoons (10 ml) liquid smoke
2 cups (480 g) ketchup
4 drops Louisiana hot sauce

Combine bell pepper, onions, honey, garlic, lemon juice, salt,
Worcestershire sauce, oatmeal stout, vinegar, liquid smoke, ketchup,
and hot sauce in a slow cooker. Set at low setting and cook for
about 5 hours, or until mixture is the consistency of ketchup. If it's
still too thin, transfer to a saucepan and reduce, uncovered, until
thickened.

Prep = 15 minutes   **Cook** = 5 hours   **Yield** = About 1 quart (946 ml)

Pilsner Pulled Pork Sandwiches

Pulled pork is a Southern staple that has become so mainstream that it can even be found in egg rolls or on pizza. The easiest way by far to make this dish is in a slow cooker. Chill it, add a little mayo and chopped celery, and you have pulled pork salad sandwiches.

3 large onions, 2 sliced in half and 1 chopped

1 pork roast (4 pounds, or 1.8 kg)

5 or 6 whole cloves

Salt and pepper

2 whole cloves garlic

3 cups (710 ml) pilsner, divided

1 bottle (16 ounces, or 455 ml) mesquite-flavored barbecue sauce

2 teaspoons (7 g) whole mustard seeds

Salt and pepper

8 crusty sandwich rolls

Coleslaw

Bread-and-butter pickles

Place one halved onion at the bottom of slow cooker. Stud pork roast with cloves and season with salt and pepper. Place roast in slow cooker on top of the onion halves. Top with the remaining onion halves (reserve chopped onion for later), and add garlic and 2 cups (475 ml) of beer to the cooker. Cover and cook at low setting for 8 to 10 hours. Remove roast and discard cloves, bone, and fat as well as any beer, onions, garlic, and fat remaining in pot. When pork roast is cool enough to handle, use a fork or your fingers to pull it apart until the entire roast is shredded.

Return the pulled pork to the slow cooker. Mix in the chopped onion, barbecue sauce, mustard seeds, salt and pepper to taste, and remaining cup of beer. Cook at high setting for 1 to 3 hours, or until onions are soft. Serve on crusty sandwich rolls topped with coleslaw and bread-and-butter pickles.

Prep = 15 minutes   **Cook** = 9 to 13 hours   **Yield** = 8 servings

Smokey Brew
Oven-Baked Beer Brisket

This recipe has existed for several generations with one variation or another. It originally called for quite a bit of seasoned salt, which can also be replaced with ready-made dry rub mixes in stores.

1 can or bottle (12 ounces, or 355 ml) beer
1 bottle (3 ½ ounces, or 104 ml) liquid smoke
1 tablespoon (15 ml) Worcestershire sauce
1 beef brisket (4 to 5 pounds, or 1.8 to 2.3 kg)
   Garlic salt
   Onion salt
   Celery salt
   Paprika
   Cracked black pepper
1 ½ cups (375 ml) Irish Whiskey Beerbecue Sauce (page 166)
   or Maple-Bacon Beerbecue Sauce (page 167)

Combine beer, liquid smoke, and Worcestershire sauce. Pour over brisket in a roasting pan. Cover and refrigerate for 8 hours or overnight. Remove from marinade and pat dry (discard marinade); wash and dry pan. Sprinkle both sides of brisket generously with garlic salt, onion salt, celery salt, paprika, and black pepper. Wrap in foil and place back in clean roasting pan. Refrigerate for another 4 to 8 hours.

Preheat oven to 250°F (120°C, or gas mark ½). Roast brisket in foil for 1 hour per pound plus 1 hour. During the last hour, open foil and pour sauce over the top, basting occasionally.

Prep = 10 minutes **Chill** = 12 to 20 hours
Cook = 5 to 6 hours **Yield** = 6 to 8 servings

Spicy Texas-Style Beerbecue Sauce

Pickling spices add a real zip to this sauce. Be sure to tie them up in a cheesecloth as one would do with a bouquet garni. This sauce works well with beef, pork, or chicken.

½ pound (225 g) pickling spices
1 teaspoon whole cloves
1 medium onion, chopped
2 stalks celery, chopped
36 ounces (1 kg) ketchup
½ cup (140 g) chili sauce
2 cans or bottles (12 ounces, or 355 ml, each) beer
1 cup (235 ml) water
½ cup (120 ml) cider vinegar
1 tablespoon (9 g) dry mustard
½ cup (120 ml) Worcestershire sauce
¾ cup (180 g) light brown sugar, firmly packed
2 teaspoons (6 g) garlic powder
1 tablespoon (18 g) salt
2 tablespoons (30 ml) lemon juice
1 tablespoon (15 ml) hot sauce

Tie pickling spices and cloves loosely in cheesecloth bag. Combine onion, celery, ketchup, chili sauce, beer, water, vinegar, dry mustard, Worcestershire sauce, brown sugar, garlic powder, salt, lemon juice, and hot sauce in stockpot, and add spice bag. Bring to a boil and then simmer for 1 ½ hours. Remove from heat, remove spice bag, and cool. Puree in food processor.

Prep = 15 minutes   **Cook** = 1½ hours
Yield = 2 to 3 cups (500 to 750 g)

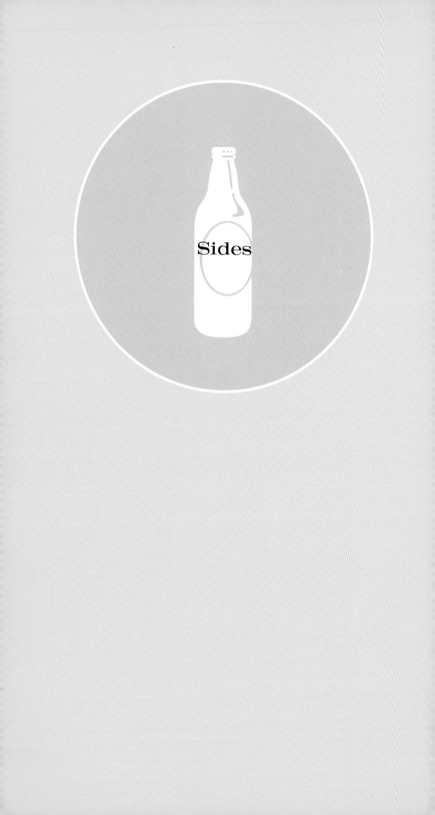

Sides

Zucchini in Beer Batter

Fried zucchini is a great side dish to serve
with Italian entrées such as *saltimbocca* or chicken
parmigiana. It also pairs well with steaks or
seafood and stands alone as an appetizer.

   1 large zucchini, or 2 small, sliced ½-inch (1.2 cm) thick
   2 teaspoons (12 g) salt, divided
   ¼ teaspoon pepper
   1 cup (125 g) all-purpose flour
1 ½ teaspoons (7 g) baking powder
   ½ teaspoon baking soda
   ½ cup (120 ml) beer
   ¼ cup (60 ml) fresh lemon juice
     Oil, for frying
     Grated Parmesan cheese

Arrange zucchini on piece of waxed paper; salt and pepper both
sides, using 1 teaspoon of salt and all the pepper. Combine flour,
baking powder, baking soda, and remaining teaspoon salt in medium
bowl. Transfer ½ cup (235 ml) of the mixture to a shallow pie plate
and dip both sides of zucchini in pie plate of flour mixture.

Stir beer and lemon juice into remaining flour mixture in bowl.
Stir until consistency of pancake batter. Heat oil in a deep fryer to
375°F (190°C). Dip breaded zucchini in beer batter and deep-fry
about four pieces at a time until crisp. Drain on paper towels and
sprinkle with Parmesan cheese.

Prep = 20 minutes   **Cook** = 10 minutes   **Yield** = 4 servings

Brussels Sprouts in Beer with Honey-Roasted Cashews

There are still people for whom the legacy of Brussels sprouts is laden with turmoil. Braising them in beer and topping them with bar-style honey-roasted cashew nuts will make most guests happy. These days, these mini cabbages are as popular at the holiday table as the pecan pie.

3 cups (709 ml) pale ale
1 clove garlic, halved
Small onion, halved
½ teaspoon salt
1 pound (455 g) Brussels sprouts
2 tablespoons (28 g) butter
½ cup (62 g) honey-roasted cashews, chopped

Bring ale, garlic, onion, and salt to a boil in a large saucepan. Add Brussels sprouts and simmer, uncovered, for 20 minutes or until tender, adding more ale if too much liquid evaporates and the pan starts to go dry. Drain liquid from Brussels sprouts and toss with butter until butter melts. Transfer to serving dish and top with chopped cashews.

Prep = 10 to 15 minutes   **Cook** = 25 minutes
Yield = 6 to 8 servings

Beer-Glazed
Baby Carrots

Beer brings out the sweetness of carrots in
an interesting way. I guarantee this side dish will
take center stage when you first try it out
on your family and friends.

1 can (12 ounces, or 355 ml) beer
1 package (16 ounces, or 455 g) fresh baby carrots
⅛ teaspoon ground cloves
⅛ teaspoon ground cinnamon
2 tablespoons (40 g) honey
2 tablespoons (28 g) butter
Grated zest and juice of ½ lemon

Bring beer, carrots, cloves, and cinnamon to a boil in a large,
covered saucepan. Cover and simmer just until carrots are tender,
8 to 10 minutes). Drain well. Add honey, butter, and lemon zest and
juice. Heat through and serve.

Prep = 5 minutes **Cook** = 10 to 12 minutes
Yield = 4 servings

Beer-Battered Baked Potato Wedges

These crunchy fried potato wedges are
made in a two-step process—first you bake them,
then you fry them—but they are worth the effort.
Serve with ketchup or honey-mustard malt vinegar
dip as a side dish or a party appetizer.

4 large baking potatoes
1 ½ cups (170 g) crushed cornflake crumbs
Ketchup (optional)
Vegetable oil, for frying

BEER BATTER:
1 egg, separated
1 ½ cup (187 g) all-purpose flour
1 can or bottle (12 ounces, or 355 ml) beer
½ teaspoon salt
½ teaspoon paprika

HONEY-MUSTARD MALT VINEGAR DIP:
1 tablespoon (15 ml) malt vinegar
1 teaspoon yellow mustard
¼ cup (85 g) honey
1 cup (225 g) mayonnaise

Preheat oven to 400°F (200°C, or gas mark 6). Bake potatoes until
nearly done, about 30 minutes. Let cool completely.

Meanwhile, prepare beer batter: Beat yolk with flour, beer, salt,
and paprika in a bowl. In a separate bowl, beat egg white until stiff
but not dry and gently fold into beer batter. Let stand for 1 hour
while potatoes are cooling.

Slice potatoes into wedges. Dip in beer batter and roll in cornflake
crumbs. Preheat deep fryer filled with oil to 375°F (190°C) and fry
potatoes until golden brown. Drain on paper towels and sprinkle
with additional salt, if desired.

For honey-mustard malt vinegar dip: Blend dip ingredients together
with a wire whisk until smooth.

Serve potato wedges hot with honey-mustard malt vinegar dip or
ketchup.

Prep = 20 minutes   **Cook** = 35 to 40 minutes
Cool/Stand = 1 hour   **Yield** = 4 to 6 servings

Beer-Battered Onion Rings

Beer-battered onion rings are (for me)
one of the most addictive foods on earth.
They are great with barbecue, steaks, and seafood,
on top of salads, and as an appetizer at parties.

- 2 cups (250 g) all-purpose flour, divided
- 1 teaspoon paprika
- ½ teaspoon cayenne
- ½ teaspoon garlic powder
- 1 teaspoon salt
- 1 bottle (12 ounces, or 355 ml) light beer
- 3 Vidalia or Spanish onions
  Vegetable oil, for frying

HONEY-BEER MUSTARD:
- ¼ cup (60 ml) beer
- ¼ cup (38 g) light brown sugar
- ¼ cup (85 g) honey
- ¼ cup (60 g) deli-style mustard
- 1 ½ cups (350 g) mayonnaise

In a large bowl, combine 1 cup (125 g) flour, paprika, cayenne, garlic powder, salt, and beer, blending well with a wire whisk. Let stand, at room temperature, for several hours or overnight.

Line a sheet or jelly-roll pan with paper toweling, place a wire cooling rack over paper, and set aside. Cut onions into ½-inch (1.2 ml) thick slices and separate into rings. Place remaining flour into a large bowl and toss a few rings in flour to coat well. Dip into beer batter, coating thoroughly, and then into the dry flour again to coat well.

Preheat a deep fryer filled with oil to 375°F (190°C) and preheat the oven to 200°F (95°C). Fry battered onions, a few at a time, until golden brown, about 2 minutes, turning once. Place on prepared pan and hold hot onion rings in preheated oven, until all have been dipped and fried. Serve with honey-beer mustard.

For honey-beer mustard: Blend beer, brown sugar, honey, mustard and mayonnaise until smooth and blended.

Prep = 20 minutes   **Stand** = 4 to 8 hours   **Cook** = 20 minutes
Yield = 6 to 8 servings

Green Bean and Portbello Mushroom Casserole with Porter

Despite—or possibly due to—a childhood full of chicken casseroles, I usually wince at the idea of opening up a can of soup for a sauce. For this updated classic green bean and mushroom casserole, use fresh French green beans and Portobello mushrooms.

1 tablespoon (30 ml) olive oil

2 tablespoon (28 g) butter, melted

1 cup (70 g) Portobello mushroom caps, coarsely chopped

1 can (10 ¾ ounces) condensed cream of mushroom soup

⅓ cup (77 g) sour cream

⅓ cup (80 ml) porter beer

⅛ teaspoon cracked pepper

1 ½ cups (150 g) French green beans, cooked

1 ⅓ cups (295 g) canned French fried onion rings

1 tablespoon (6 g) grated Parmesan cheese

In a medium-size nonstick skillet, melt butter with olive oil and sauté mushrooms until tender. Stir in soup, sour cream, beer, and pepper. Arrange beans in a medium-size casserole dish and cover with soup mixture. Top with onion rings and sprinkle with cheese.

Preheat oven to 400°F (200°C, or gas mark 6). Bake for 18 to 25 minutes or until topping is golden. Note: Add additional time if casserole is refrigerated before baking.

Prep = 10 minutes **Cook** = 25 to 32 minutes
Yield = 6 servings

Broccoli, Blue Cheese, and Beer Bake

This is a great make-ahead side dish for company. After preparing, just cover and refrigerate overnight. If baking directly from the refrigerator, remember to increase the cooking time by ten minutes.

1 ½ pounds (680 g) broccoli
  Boiling salted water
4 tablespoons (55 g) butter
¼ cup (40 g) finely chopped onion
¼ cup (31 g) all-purpose flour
¼ teaspoon garlic salt
1 package (3 ounces, or 85 g) cream cheese, softened
½ cup (60 g) crumbled blue cheese
1 cup (235 ml) half-and-half
1 can or bottle (12 ounces, or 355 ml) beer
¼ cup (25 g) sliced ripe olives, well drained
⅓ cup (33 g) crushed butter-flavor crackers
2 tablespoons (10 g) grated Parmesan cheese

Rinse broccoli well. Drain. Cut tops into bite-size florets and trim off ends of stems. Peel lower portions of remaining stems. Slice stems into ¼-inch (6 mm) pieces. Cook florets and stems in boiling salted water for 4 to 6 minutes, until tender-crisp. Drain. Place in a shallow, greased 2-quart (1.8 L) casserole.

Preheat oven to 350°F (180°C, or gas mark 4). In a medium saucepan, melt butter over medium heat. Add onions. Cook until soft but not browned. Stir in flour and garlic salt. Cook, stirring, until bubbly. Remove pan from heat. Mix in cream cheese and blue cheese with a wire whisk. Gradually blend in half-and-half and beer, cook stirring constantly until mixture thickens and bubbles. Stir in olives. Pour over broccoli. Combine cracker crumbs with Parmesan cheese and sprinkle over casserole.

Bake for 20 to 25 minutes, until heated through and topping is lightly browned.

Prep = 20 minutes   **Cook** = 40 minutes   **Yield** = 6 servings

Pale Ale au Gratin Potatoes

Adding beer to any au gratin dish actually helps the sauce get more of a golden brown glaze. This is a great recipe to serve with baked ham or roast beef for holiday meals.

3 tablespoons (42 g) butter
¼ cup (40 g) chopped onion
2 tablespoons (16 g) all-purpose flour
½ teaspoon salt
¼ teaspoon pepper
1 ¼ cups (295 ml) half-and-half
1 bottle or can (12 ounces, or 355 ml) pale ale
2 cups (225 g) shredded white Cheddar cheese, divided
6 medium potatoes, sliced wafer thin
¼ cup (30 g) dried bread crumbs
2 tablespoons (10 g) grated Parmesan cheese

Preheat oven to 375°F (190°C, or gas mark 5). Spray a 1½ quart (1.4 L) casserole with nonstick cooking spray. In a 2-quart saucepan over medium heat, sauté onion in butter until tender, stirring occasionally (about 2 minutes). Blend in flour, salt and pepper. Cook, stirring constantly, until bubbling; remove from heat.

Blend in half-and-half and beer. Heat to boiling, stirring constantly with a wire whisk until mixture comes to a boil. Boil one minute and stir in 1½ cups (170 g) of cheese until melted.

Spread potatoes in casserole. Pour cheese sauce over potatoes. Bake uncovered for 1 hour. In a small bowl, mix bread crumbs with remaining ½ cup (55 g) of cheese and Parmesan cheese. Sprinkle over potatoes and bake 15 minutes longer or until topping is brown and bubbling.

Prep = 20 minutes   **Cook** = 1 ½ hours   **Yield** = 6 servings

Pilsner Mashed Potatoes with Parsley, Chives, and Cheddar Cheese

Because pilsner is a pale-colored, mild beer, try adding some to the cooking water of mashed potatoes. It gives an interesting flavor to the subtle dish without overpowering it.

2 pounds (905 g) Idaho potatoes, peeled and cubed
2 cloves garlic, peeled and sliced in half
1 bottle (12 ounces, or 355 ml) pilsner
3 tablespoons (42 g) butter
¼ cup (82 g) sour cream
½ cup (120 ml) milk, heated
¾ cup (90 g) shredded Cheddar cheese
1 tablespoon (4 g) minced fresh chives
1 tablespoon (4 g) minced parsley
Salt and pepper

Place potatoes in a large saucepan and add garlic and pilsner. Add enough water to the pan to cover potatoes. Bring to a boil, then reduce heat slightly and cook for 20 to 30 minutes, or until tender. Drain potatoes well in a colander. Remove garlic cloves. Be sure saucepan is completely dry and melt butter in it over low heat. Remove from heat and return warm potatoes to the saucepan. Begin mashing with a handheld potato masher. Add sour cream, hot milk, Cheddar cheese, chives, and parsley. Continue mashing until no longer lumpy. Season with salt and pepper to taste.

Prep = 15 minutes   **Cook** = 25 to 35 minutes
Yield = 4 servings

Spinach Risotto with Pilsner and Peas

Risotto is a labor of love because,
unlike other rice, you can't walk away
from the stove and leave it unattended. It needs
constant nurturing and stirring. It's really
not difficult once you become familiar
with the technique.

2 cans (14 ounces, or 425 ml, each) chicken broth
1 bottle (12 ounces, or 355 ml) pilsner
1 ¼ cups (285 ml) water
1 bay leaf
3 tablespoons (45 ml) olive oil
2 cloves garlic, crushed
1 onion, finely chopped
1 cup (195 g) uncooked Arborio rice
1 package (10 ounces, or 280 g) frozen chopped spinach, thawed and squeezed dry
1 package (10 ounces, or 280 g) frozen peas, thawed and drained
½ cup (50 g) grated Parmesan cheese
2 tablespoons (28 g) butter
Salt and pepper

In a small saucepan, bring broth, pilsner, and water to a simmer with bay leaf. Keep warm over low heat. In a medium saucepan over medium heat, sauté garlic and onion in olive oil until softened, 3 to 5 minutes. Add rice and cook, stirring until coated, 1 to 2 minutes. Add ½ cup (120 ml) of warm broth, stirring until absorbed (about 1 minute). Add 2 cups (475 ml) more of broth mixture. Reduce heat to a low simmer and stir until liquid is absorbed. Continue adding liquid about 1 cup (235 ml) at a time, stirring, until a creamy consistency is reached, when rice is tender, and there is little liquid left in the pan. (The process should take 20 to 25 minutes and you may not need all of the broth mixture.) Stir in spinach, peas, Parmesan cheese, and butter until blended and heated through. Season with salt and pepper to taste.

Prep = 15 minutes   **Cook** = 30 to 35 minutes
Yield = 4 to 6 servings

Belgian Dilled New Potatoes

New potatoes simmered in a lambic are the perfect accompaniment for any seafood dish. Cover and chill leftovers—if there are any!—to serve as potato salad.

12 small new potatoes, scrubbed
1 bottle (12 ounces, or 355 ml) Blue Moon
2 cups (475 ml) water
3 tablespoons (42 g) butter
1 clove garlic, crushed
1 minced shallot
1 tablespoon (2 g) minced fresh dill
1 tablespoon (4 g) minced fresh parsley
Salt and pepper

Use a vegetable peeler to peel off a strip of skin around the sides of each potato. Put potatoes, beer, and water in a medium saucepan and bring to a boil. Reduce heat to medium, cover, and cook until potatoes are tender, about 30 minutes. Drain off liquid from potatoes in a colander. In a medium skillet over medium heat, melt butter and sauté garlic and shallot until tender, about 4 minutes. Turn down heat; add potatoes, dill, and parsley, then gently shake around in pan to coat with butter. Season to taste with salt and pepper.

Prep = 10 minutes **Cook** = 35 minutes **Yield** = 4 servings

Green Beans with Portobello Mushrooms and Porter

I like to accent my Asian-inspired dishes with these beans on the side. Chop and sprinkle some fresh scallions on top for an Eastern touch.

1 ½ pounds (680 g) French green beans
¼ teaspoon baking soda
⅓ cup (41 g) slivered almonds
8 ounces (225 g) sliced portobello mushrooms
1 tablespoon (15 ml) olive oil
1 tablespoon (14 g) butter
¼ cup (60 ml) porter

In a large saucepan, bring 1 quart (1 L) of water to a boil with baking soda. Trim green beans and add to boiling water. Cook for 6 to 8 minutes, or until tender-crisp. Immediately rinse under cold water to stop cooking and allow to drain.

Meanwhile, in a small but heavy nonstick skillet, stir-fry almonds until they turn a toasty golden brown (no oil needed).

Cut slices of portobello mushrooms into four sections each. In a medium skillet over medium heat, melt oil and butter. Sauté mushrooms for 3 minutes, add porter, and reduce until most of the liquid has evaporated. Gently stir in green beans to heat through, and toss with almonds.

Prep = 15 minutes   **Cook** = 20 minutes   **Yield** = 6 servings

Brunch

Bacon, Tomato, Beer, and Cheese Brunch Pie

Because of the buttery cracker crust,
this isn't exactly your typical quiche. This will serve
six people for brunch but will go much further if you
decide to bake it as an appetizer for a party.

CRACKER CRUST:
Nonstick cooking spray
1 ½ cups (150 g) crushed saltine crackers (36 crackers)
¼ cup (55 g) melted butter

FILLING:
2 tablespoons (28 g) butter
1 ½ cups (240 g) chopped onions
1 can (15 ounces, or 425 g) diced tomatoes, well drained
2 cups (225 g) shredded sharp Cheddar cheese, divided
⅓ cup (27 g) crisp crumbled cooked bacon
½ cup (120 ml) beer
½ cup (120 ml) half-and-half
½ teaspoon salt
¼ teaspoon pepper
3 large eggs
⅓ cup (33 g) thinly sliced scallions

Preheat oven to 325°F (170°C, or gas mark 3). Spray a 9-inch (22.5 cm) glass pie plate with nonstick cooking spray.

For cracker crust: Combine crushed crackers with melted butter, and press crumb mixture into the bottom and sides of the prepared pie plate.

For filling: Melt butter in a nonstick skillet and sauté onions until transparent and most of the moisture has evaporated. Add tomatoes and continue cooking for about 2 more minutes. Spoon mixture into cracker crust. Top with 1 ½ cups (170 g) of cheese and the bacon. Beat together beer, half-and-half, salt, pepper, and eggs in a bowl. Pour over cheese in crust.

Bake for 40 minutes. Top with remaining ½ cup (55 g) of cheese and sprinkle with scallions. Return to oven for 5 more minutes, then serve immediately.

Prep = 20 minutes   **Cook** = 45 minutes   **Yield** = 6 to 8 servings

Eggs Beeradict

Traditionally, eggs Benedict are topped with hollandaise—the drama queen of sauces. If it gets just a little too hot, it curdles. Some restaurants solve the problem by serving a mock eggs Benedict with a cheese-based sauce. It helps take the headache out of hollandaise.

 4 tablespoons (55 g) butter
¼ cup (31 g) all-purpose flour
¼ teaspoon salt
⅛ teaspoon dry mustard
 1 cup (235 ml) half-and-half
 1 can (12 ounces, or 355 ml) beer
 1 cup (115 g) shredded Cheddar cheese
 4 English muffins, split in half and toasted
 8 slices Canadian bacon, grilled
 8 eggs, poached
   Paprika
 4 pitted ripe olives, sliced in half lengthwise

Melt butter in a large saucepan over medium heat and blend in flour, salt, and dry mustard. Blend in half-and-half and beer with a wire whisk and cook, stirring constantly, until the sauce thickens and comes to a boil. Blend in cheese until melted.

Assemble English muffins on plates, top with Canadian bacon slices, poached eggs, and cheese sauce. Dust with paprika and top each egg with an olive half.

Prep = 30 minutes   **Cook** = 30 minutes   **Yield** = 4 servings

Chocolate Bock
French Toast

Bread and chocolate is as classic a combination
as beer and chocolate is novel. Chocolate bock adds
a subtle, surprising dimension to this French toast.

  6 eggs
½ cup (120 ml) heavy cream
½ cup (120 ml) chocolate bock beer
  2 teaspoons (10 ml) vanilla extract
½ teaspoon ground cinnamon
   Butter
  1 loaf country-style bread, sliced into 1-inch (2.5 cm) thick slices
   Confectioners' sugar

CHOCOLATE BOCK SYRUP:
1 ½ cups (355 ml) maple syrup
½ cup (120 ml) chocolate bock

In a large bowl, beat eggs, cream, beer, vanilla, and cinnamon until
well blended. Heat a large nonstick skillet or griddle over medium
heat. Dip bread slices in egg batter. Lightly butter pan with 1 tablespoon (14 g) of butter at a time as needed. Sauté bread slices on
each side until golden brown. Sprinkle with confectioners' sugar.
Serve with chocolate bock syrup.

For chocolate bock syrup: Combine maple syrup with chocolate
bock in a medium saucepan and simmer until slightly thickened.

Prep = 15 minutes **Cook** = 20 minutes **Yield** = 6 servings

Irish Rabbit

It's only logical that the Irish version of this
classic English dish would be prepared with stout.
I like to use potato bread toast and Irish bacon to
make it even more authentic, but it is just as good
with toasted French bread and Canadian bacon.

- 4 tablespoons (55 g) butter
- ¼ cup (31 g) all-purpose flour
- 1 cup (235 ml) milk
- 2 teaspoons (5 g) Dijon mustard
- 1 tablespoon (20 g) honey
- 1 cup (235 ml) Guinness Stout
- 2 cups (225 g) shredded Cheddar cheese
- Salt and pepper
- Toasted potato bread
- 8 slices Irish bacon, grilled

Melt the butter in a large saucepan over medium heat, and blend in
flour with a wire whisk to make a smooth bubbly paste or roux.
Cook over a low heat for about a minute until smooth and bubbling,
but don't allow to brown. Remove pan from heat and gradually beat
the milk into the roux. Return to heat and stir until the mixture
thickens. Blend in mustard and honey and finally the Guinness.
Cook, whisking constantly, until mixture thickens, then add shredded
cheese. Continue whisking over low heat only until all the cheese
has melted. Season with salt and pepper to taste. Arrange toast on
four ovenproof plates. Cover toast with Irish bacon and spoon rabbit
over the top. Run each plate under the broiler until rabbit is puffy
and golden.

Prep = 15 minutes **Cook** = 20 minutes **Yield** = 4 servings

Beer and Sausage Strata

This is an all-time favorite do-ahead brunch dish. Versions of it appear in Junior League and church cookbooks across the country. You really only need to chill it for one hour. It's so easy to prepare the night before—that's the appeal.

½ pound (225 g) sausage meat
½ cup (75 g) seeded and chopped red bell pepper
8 slices home-style white bread, crusts removed, cut into ½-inch (1.2 cm) cubes
¾ pound (340 g) Monterey Jack cheese, shredded, divided
4 eggs, beaten lightly
1 cup (235 ml) half-and-half
1 cup (235 ml) beer
½ teaspoon salt
½ teaspoon onion powder
1 teaspoon Dijon mustard
2 tablespoons (8 g) snipped fresh parsley
½ teaspoon Worcestershire sauce
3 tablespoons (42 g) unsalted butter, melted and cooled slightly

In a skillet, brown sausage with bell pepper over medium heat, breaking it up with a fork, and with a slotted spoon transfer to paper towels to drain. Brush a 1-quart (1 L) soufflé dish with some of the fat remaining in the skillet. Arrange a third of the bread cubes in the bottom of the dish and sprinkle them with one-third of the cheese. Top the cheese with all the sausage; top the sausage with half the remaining bread. Sprinkle half the remaining cheese over the bread. Top the strata with the remaining bread and press the layers together slightly.

In a bowl, whisk together the eggs, half-and-half, beer, salt, onion powder, mustard, parsley, and Worcestershire sauce. Pour the mixture over the strata and sprinkle the top with the remaining cheese. Drizzle the top with the melted butter and chill, covered, for at least 1 hour or overnight.

Preheat oven to 350°F (180°C, or gas mark 4). Remove the strata from the refrigerator and let it stand at room temperature for 45 minutes. Put the dish in a baking pan and add enough hot water to the pan to reach halfway up the sides of the dish. Bake the strata for 1 hour and 15 minutes, or until golden brown and set.

Prep = 20 minutes   **Cool/Stand** = 45 minutes to 1 hour
Cook = 1 hour 25 minutes   **Yield** = 6 servings

Beer, Cheese, and Chive Soufflé

Nothing could be more temperamental
or impressive than a soufflé. Adding beer helps
make it a little puffier but you'll still need to make
that gently paced dash to the dining room table.

4 tablespoons (55 g) butter, plus more for greasing pan

¼ cup (31 g) all-purpose flour

½ teaspoon salt

⅛ teaspoon paprika

½ cup (120 ml) beer

½ cup (120 ml) half-and-half

1 cup (115 g) shredded Cheddar cheese

2 tablespoons (10 g) grated Parmesan cheese

1 tablespoon (4 g) snipped fresh chives

3 large eggs, separated

Fold a sheet of aluminum foil to form a triple-thickness 4-inch
(10 cm) wide band that will overlap the circumference of a 1-quart
(1 L) soufflé dish by 2 inches (5 cm). Butter the inside of the soufflé
dish and one side of the foil. Extend the dish 3 inches (7.5 cm)
higher by securing the band, butter side in, around the dish with
a piece of tape.

Preheat oven to 350°F (180°C, or gas mark 4). In a medium
saucepan, melt butter over medium heat and blend in flour, salt,
and paprika, whisking with a wire whisk to make a smooth bubbly
paste or roux. Blend in beer and half-and-half, and cook, whisking
constantly, until sauce has thickened. Remove from heat and blend
in cheeses and chives until smooth and melted.

In a medium bowl with an electric mixer, beat egg yolks until thick
and lemon colored (about 3 minutes at high speed). In a separate
bowl with an electric mixer, beat egg whites until stiff but not dry.
Blend egg yolks into cheese mixture, then blend about one-quarter
of egg whites into cheese mixture. Finally, fold cheese mixture into
remaining egg whites, taking care not to "deflate." Pour carefully
into soufflé dish.

Bake for 50 to 60 minutes, or until a knife inserted about 1 inch
(2.5 cm) from the edge comes out clean. Carefully remove foil band.
Serve immediately.

Prep = 20 minutes   **Cook** = 58 to 68 minutes
Yield = 2 to 4 servings

Stout and Sweet Potato Waffles

This is one of those breakfast/brunch items that are good enough for dessert. Try serving the waffles with praline ice cream and caramel sauce. Sweet potatoes or yams can be used interchangeably.

1 ½ cups (187 g) all-purpose flour
1 teaspoon (4.6 g) baking powder
½ teaspoon salt
½ teaspoon ground cinnamon
½ teaspoon ground ginger
½ teaspoon grated nutmeg
¼ teaspoon ground cardamom
3 eggs, separated
½ cup (120 ml) milk
½ cup (120 ml) Guinness Stout
2 tablespoons (30 ml) bourbon
1 cup (225 g) mashed cooked sweet potatoes or yams, cooled
2 tablespoons (28 g) melted butter
Maple syrup, heated, for serving
Whipped butter, for serving

Sift together flour, baking powder, salt, and spices. Beat the egg yolks and mix them in a separate bowl with the milk, stout, bourbon, sweet potatoes, and melted butter. Beat into the flour mixture. Beat the egg whites in a separate bowl until they form soft peaks, and fold them into the batter. Bake in a nonstick waffle iron, following manufacturer's instructions for plain waffles. Serve with hot maple syrup and whipped butter.

Prep = 20 minutes   **Cook** = 25 to 35 minutes
Yield = 6 to 9 waffles

Blueberry-Buckwheat Beer Pancakes

Whenever I think of blueberry buckwheat pancakes, I remember my trips to Maine that always included lobster rolls, fiddlehead ferns, fresh blueberries, and honking at moose in the road.

2 cups (240 g) buckwheat flour

½ cup (115 g) light brown sugar, firmly packed

1 ½ teaspoons (7 g) baking powder

¼ teaspoon salt

12 ounces (355 ml) flat porter

½ cup (120 ml) light cream

¼ cup (55 g) melted butter

2 eggs, lightly beaten

1 teaspoon vanilla extract

¼ teaspoon ground cinnamon

⅛ teaspoon grated nutmeg

1 pint (455 g) fresh blueberries, washed and well dried

Whipped butter, for serving

Blueberry syrup, for serving

Combine buckwheat flour, brown sugar, baking powder, and salt in a bowl. In separate bowl, combine porter, cream, melted butter, beaten egg, vanilla, cinnamon, and nutmeg. Slowly stir egg mixture into dry ingredients. Mix gently, taking care not to beat batter.

Preheat a nonstick griddle or large nonstick skillet over medium heat. LIghtly coat with oil. Pour batter by ⅓ cupfuls (80 g) onto the griddle or large skillet, scattering a few blueberries onto each pancake. When large bubbles form on the uncooked surface of the pancakes, they are ready to turn. Flip and cook for another minute and a half. Repeat with remaining batter. Serve warm with whipped butter and hot blueberry syrup.

Prep = 15 minutes   **Cook** = 12 to 15 minutes   **Yield** = 4 servings

California Monterey Jack Rabbit

This is a California spin on the British classic brunch dish, featuring Monterey Jack Cheese, avocados, and mushrooms. Any light-colored lager will work well.

4 tablespoons (55 g) butter, divided
½ cup (120 ml) beer
2 ½ cups (287 g) shredded Monterey Jack cheese, divided
1 tablespoon (15 ml) Worcestershire sauce
1 large egg, lightly beaten
2 cups (140 g) sliced mushrooms
1 clove garlic, crushed
Whole wheat toast points or triangles
1 large ripe avocado, pitted, peeled, and sliced
¼ cup (33 g) sliced ripe olives

Melt 1 tablespoon (14 g) of butter in the top of a double boiler over simmering water. Add beer and heat until warm. Stir in 2 cups (230 g) of cheese and Worcestershire sauce and whisk until smooth and melted. Beat a little into the egg and then blend the egg mixture back into the cheese mixture and heat through. Remove double boiler from burner and set to the side of the stove to keep warm.

Meanwhile, melt remaining butter in a nonstick skillet and sauté mushrooms with garlic until tender and browned. Arrange toast points in individual ovenproof casseroles. Divide mushroom mixture over toast points and top with slices of avocado. Spoon rabbit evenly over mushrooms. Sprinkle with remaining cheese and garnish with olives. Broil until golden and bubbling.

Prep = 20 minutes   **Cook** = 10 to 12 minutes   **Yield** = 4 servings

Classic Welsh Rabbit

Welsh "rabbit" (sometimes spelled "rarebit") is a traditional favorite found throughout the United Kingdom and was a popular brunch item when I was growing up in the United States. In this context, the rabbit is a beer-based cheese sauce that can be served over English muffins, toast, even crumpets. Any beer will work well, but I like to use British ale.

1 tablespoon (14 g) butter
1 cup (235 ml) ale
2 cups (225 g) shredded Cheddar cheese
½ teaspoon dry mustard
½ teaspoon paprika
1 teaspoon Worcestershire sauce
Salt and pepper
4 English muffins, split in half and toasted
8 thin slices tomato, seeded and well drained
8 strips cooked bacon

In the top of a double boiler over simmering water, melt butter. Add ale. Cook over hot (not boiling) water until beer is warm. Blend in shredded Cheddar with a wire whisk until it melts. Stir in dry mustard, paprika, Worcestershire sauce, and salt and pepper to taste.

Arrange English muffins on four ovenproof plates, spoon sauce evenly over muffins, and top with tomato slices. Run plates under broiler until rabbit is puffy and lightly browned. Garnish with bacon strips.

Prep = 10 minutes   **Cook** = 12 to 14 minutes   **Yield** = 4 servings

Bourbon Street Brunch Eggs with Beer

A dish called Eggs Portuguese inspired this recipe. I always ordered it for brunch when I was dining at any number of restaurants in the French Quarter of New Orleans. The eggs were served over puff pastry topped with a tomato-ham mixture.

½ cup (50 g) finely chopped fresh mushrooms
½ cup (75 g) finely chopped fully cooked ham
½ cup (50 g) finely chopped green onions
2 cloves garlic, minced
1 can (15 ounces, or 425 g) diced tomatoes, drained
2 tablespoons (28 g) butter
2 tablespoons (16 g) all-purpose flour
⅛ teaspoon cayenne
1 can (12 ounces, or 355 ml) beer
4 frozen puff pastry patty shells, baked crisp (do not cut open "lids")
8 eggs, poached
Snipped fresh parsley

HOLLANDAISE SAUCE:
3 egg yolks
Juice of ½ lemon
1 teaspoon cold water
1 teaspoon salt
1 teaspoon ground black pepper
½ cup (112 g) soft butter

In a medium nonstick skillet over medium heat, sauté mushrooms, chopped ham, green onions, garlic, and tomatoes in butter until vegetables are tender. Blend in flour and cayenne. Reduce heat to low, blend in beer, and cook, stirring occasionally, for 20 minutes, until reduced and thickened.

For hollandaise sauce: In the top of a double boiler over simmering water, whisk together egg yolks, lemon juice, cold water, salt, and pepper. Gradually whisk butter into yolk mixture while cooking over simmering water Continue whisking over low heat for 8 minutes, or until sauce is thickened. Serve immediately. If sauce breaks down, re-emulsify with a few drops of lemon juice or cold water.

Split open each patty shell horizontally, across the middle, and arrange so that cut sides are facing up on each plate. Spoon mushroom mixture onto patty shell halves and top with poached eggs. Spoon hollandaise sauce over eggs and sprinkle with snipped parsley.

Prep = 20 minutes   **Cook** = 30 to 40 minutes   **Yield** = 4 servings

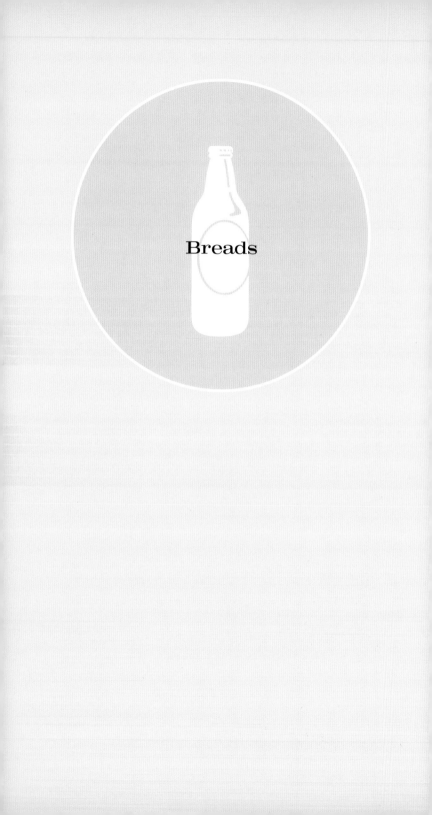

Breads

Sun-Dried Tomato, Olive, and Basil Beer Bread

Planning an afternoon tea? This bread
is a great vehicle for cream cheese sandwiches.
It's also nice to serve with a pasta meal, in
place of bread sticks or Italian bread.

3 ½ cups (438 g) all-purpose flour

1 teaspoon salt

½ teaspoon baking soda

1 teaspoon baking powder

1 large egg, lightly beaten

1 can or bottle (12 ounces, or 355 ml) light-colored lager

½ cup (25 g) sun-dried tomatoes, packed
(reserve 1 tablespoon, or 15 ml oil)

1 tablespoon (5 g) fresh minced basil, or 1 teaspoon dried

⅓ cup (43 g) sliced green pimiento-stuffed olives, well drained

Preheat the oven to 350°F (180°C, or gas mark 4). Grease and flour
9 × 5-inch (22.5 × 13 cm) loaf pan.

In a large bowl, whisk together the flour, salt, baking soda, and
baking powder. Add the egg, beer, tomatoes with the reserved oil,
basil, and olives. Stir until just combined; do not overmix. Turn the
batter into the pan and bake the bread in the middle of the oven for
40 minutes, or until a tester comes out clean. Let cool 15 minutes on
a wire rack before inverting to remove from pan. Cool completely
before trying to slice.

Prep = 15 minutes   **Cook** = 40 minutes   **Yield** = 1 loaf

Banana Beer Bread

To give this banana bread the most character, you'll want to choose a dark beer, such as stout or porter. This is essentially like the recipe Grandma used to make when I was a child. I didn't realize at the time that it was beer that made the difference.

½ cup (112 g) mashed banana
½ cup (115 g) brown sugar, firmly packed
¼ cup (50 g) granulated sugar
1 egg
1 teaspoon vanilla extract
1 tablespoon (15 ml) vegetable oil
1 cup (125 g) all-purpose flour
1 cup (120 g) whole wheat flour
1 teaspoon baking soda
½ teaspoon salt
1 teaspoon ground cinnamon
¼ teaspoon ground cloves
¼ teaspoon grated nutmeg
½ teaspoon ground ginger
1 cup (235 ml) stout or porter
1 cup (125 g) toasted chopped pecans
1 cup (165 g) golden raisins, packed

Preheat oven to 350°F (180°C, or gas mark 4). In a medium bowl, combine mashed banana, brown sugar, granulated sugar, egg, vanilla, and oil. Sift together all-purpose flour, wheat flour, baking soda, salt, cinnamon, cloves, nutmeg, and ginger. Add flour mixture to mashed banana mixture alternately with beer, ending with flour mixture. Fold in pecans and raisins.

Pour batter into a 9 × 5-inch (22.5 × 13 cm) loaf pan and bake for 1 hour. Cool in pan for 15 minutes and then invert onto cooling rack.

Prep = 20 minutes   **Cook** = 1 hour   **Yield** = 1 loaf

Beer Bread Sticks

Homemade bread sticks are so satisfying
to make. This recipe features a fennel-flavored
dough. However, you can vary the flavor with
garlic and herbs such as rosemary or basil.

1 envelope (¼ ounce, or 7 g) dry active yeast
¾ cup (175 ml) warm water, 110°F to 115°F (43°C to 46°C)
1 teaspoon sugar
¾ cup (175 ml) beer, at room temperature
¾ cup (175 ml) olive oil, plus extra for bowl
4 ½ cups (563 g) all-purpose flour
1 ½ teaspoons (9 g) salt
1 tablespoon (7 g) fennel seeds
Cornmeal

In a large bowl, combine yeast, water, and sugar until mixture
bubbles. Blend in beer, olive oil, flour, salt, and fennel seeds. Knead
dough for 4 to 5 minutes, or until smooth and elastic. Place dough
in oiled bowl, turning to coat dough with oil. Cover with towel and let
rise in a warm place until doubled.

Preheat oven to 350°F (180°C, or gas mark 4). On a cornmeal-
floured board, roll out dough ¼-inch (6-mm) thick and cut into
strips. Stretch on a nonstick baking sheet until 8-inches (20-cm)
long. Bake for 20 to 30 minutes, or until golden and crisp.

Prep = 15 minutes   **Rise** = 1 hour
Cook = 20 to 30 minutes   **Yield** = About 2 dozen bread sticks

Flower Pot Porter
Pecan Bread

When baking bread in flowerpots, always
use pots that have never been used for planting.

    3 6-inch (15 cm) terra-cotta flowerpots, cleaned
    2 teaspoons (9 g) baking soda
    1 cup (178 g) pitted, chopped dates
    ½ cup (90 g) raisins, packed
    2 cups (475 ml) porter
    3 tablespoons (42 g) butter
    ½ cup (120 ml) maple syrup
    ½ cup (170 g) molasses
    1 tablespoon (6 g) grated orange peel
    2 teaspoons (30 ml) orange extract
    2 eggs
    4 cups (480 g) whole wheat pastry flour
    1 cup (125 g) toasted chopped pecans (see Note)

Wash and dry three flowerpots so no residual moisture remains in
the clay. (Dry them for 15 minutes in a 350°F [180°C, or gas mark 4]
oven and allow to cool.) Line flower pots with aluminum foil; spray
the insides with nonstick cooking spray containing flour. In a bowl,
coat dates and raisins with baking soda. Heat porter in a saucepan
and bring to a boil. Remove from heat and pour over dates and
raisins. Set aside to cool.

   In a large mixing bowl, cream together butter, maple syrup,
molasses, orange peel, orange extract, and eggs. Stir in flour. Add
nuts and cooled date and raisin mixture. Spoon batter into flower
pots, filling only half way.

   Preheat oven to 350°F (180°C, or gas mark 4). Stand flowerpots
upright on cookie sheet and bake for 45 to 50 minutes. Look for
tops of breads to split, and test for doneness with a toothpick. Do
not cut bread until thoroughly cooled. Peel away the foil then return
bread to flowerpots before presenting them as gifts or at the table.

To toast pecans: Preheat oven to 350°F (180°C, or gas mark 4)
and spread pecans on a baking sheet. Bake for 6 to 8 minutes,
stirring once or twice, until evenly golden brown. Watch carefully
to avoid burning.

Prep = 20 minutes   **Cook** = 1 hour to 1 hour 10 minutes
Yield = 3 breads

Beer, Bacon, and Cheddar Corn Bread

Bacon and cheddar make this corn bread hearty enough to serve as a lunchtime sandwich substitute, along with a cup of soup. It's especially good with potato soup or corn chowder.

1 ½ cups (187 g) all-purpose flour
½ cup (69 g) yellow cornmeal
2 tablespoons (25 g) sugar
1 ½ teaspoons (7 g) baking powder
¾ teaspoon baking soda
½ teaspoon salt
1 cup (235 ml) beer
2 eggs
⅓ cup (78 ml) vegetable oil
2 cups (225 g) Cheddar cheese, shredded
⅓ cup (23 g) crisp crumbled cooked bacon

Preheat oven to 350°F (180°C, or gas mark 4). Grease a 9 × 5-inch (22.5 × 13 cm) loaf pan. In a medium bowl, blend together flour, cornmeal, sugar, baking powder, baking soda, and salt. In a separate bowl, beat together beer, eggs, olive oil, cheese, and bacon. Slowly blend wet ingredients into dry ingredients, mixing just until blended. Batter should be lumpy; do not overmix. Pour into prepared pan. Bake for 45 minutes to 1 hour, or until a toothpick inserted comes out clean. Cool in pan for 15 minutes and then invert over rack and remove from pan.

Prep = 20 minutes   **Cook** = 1 hour   **Yield** = 1 loaf

Beer Rye Bread

This makes a great loaf for sandwich bread,
whether it's a ham and cheese, a grilled Reuben,
or smoked chicken, cucumber, and watercress.
A beer-based rye bread complements
just about any cold cuts.

2¼ to 2¾ cups (281 to 344 g) all-purpose flour, divided
1¼ cups (160 g) rye flour
¾ cup (175 ml) dark beer, such as stout, bock or porter
3 tablespoons (60 g) honey
1 tablespoon (14 g) butter, softened
2 envelopes (¼ ounce, or 7 g, each) dry active yeast
½ cup (120 ml) warm water, 110°F to 115°F (43°C to 46°C)
2 teaspoons (4 g) caraway seeds
2 teaspoons (12 g) salt
½ teaspoon garlic powder
vegetable oil

Mix 1½ cups (188 g) of the flour with the rye flour. Heat beer, honey,
and butter slightly. Dissolve yeast in warm water in large bowl.
Add beer mixture, caraway seeds, salt, garlic powder, and 1½ cups
(188 g) of the flour mixture. Beat until smooth. Add remaining all-
purpose flour. Knead 4 minutes, adding more all-purpose flour, if
necessary. Shape into ball. Place into 8-inch (20-cm) round pan,
greased. Oil top of loaf. Flatten to fit pan. Allow to rise for 1½ hours.

Preheat oven to 375°F (190°C, or gas mark 5). Bake for 30
minutes. Remove from pan after cooling 15 minutes and continue
cool on rack.

Prep = 20 minutes   **Rise** = 1½ hours   **Cook** = 30 minutes
Yield = 1 loaf

Easy Beer Batter Bread

The original recipe for this was even easier because it called for self-rising flour, which is nothing more than all-purpose flour with the addition of baking powder and salt. However, most of us don't keep a bag of it on the shelf, so I've adapted the recipe so that anyone who has basic ingredients on hand can bake this without making a special trek to the store.

⅓ cup (65 g) sugar
1 ½ teaspoons (6.9 g) baking powder
1 ½ teaspoons (9 g) salt
3 cups (375 g) all-purpose flour
1 can (12 ounces, or 355 ml) flat beer, at room temperature
3 tablespoons (42 g) butter, softened

Preheat oven to 350°F (180°C, or gas mark 4). Combine sugar with baking soda and salt. Mix into flour. Stir in beer. Grease and flour a 9 × 5-inch (22.5 × 13 cm) loaf pan. Spread batter in pan. Bake for 40 minutes. Remove from oven and spread the top of the loaf with butter. Return to oven and bake for another 20 minutes. Cool in pan for 15 minutes. Invert over rack and remove from pan; let cool before slicing.

Prep = 10 minutes   **Cook** = 1 hour
Yield = 1 loaf

Classic Beer Biscuits

Beer leavens traditional baking powder biscuits, making them lighter and baking to a golden brown. No biscuit cutter? Remove the top of an empty beer can with an opener. The can's sharp rim makes a perfect biscuit shape.

6 cups (750 g) all-purpose flour, plus extra for kneading
2 teaspoons (9.2 g) baking powder
1 teaspoon salt
⅓ cup (75 g) shortening
⅓ cup (75 g) butter, softened
1 cup less 1 tablespoon (220 g) beer

Combine flour, baking powder, and salt. Sift together twice into a medium bowl. Add shortening and butter. Cut with a pastry blender until mixture resembles cornmeal. Stir in beer with a fork and gather into two balls. Knead each ball very lightly—do not overwork. Dust each with flour and roll out to a ½-inch (1.2 cm) thickness. Cut with a 2 ½-inch (6.2 cm) round biscuit cutter.

Preheat oven to 450°F (230°C, or gas mark 8). Place biscuits on an ungreased nonstick baking sheet and bake for 10 minutes, until golden brown.

Prep = 25 minutes   **Cook** = 10 minutes   **Yield** = About 30 biscuits

Stout Garlic and Herb Flatbread

Flatbreads and beer were made for each other.
This simple dough is even simpler when you don't
have to dissolve an envelope of yeast. Herbs can vary
according to your imagination, even using
fresh ones from the garden, if available.

1 clove garlic, crushed

3 tablespoons (45 ml) olive oil

2 cups (250 g) all-purpose flour, plus extra for kneading

1 teaspoon salt

¾ cup (175 ml) Guinness Stout

Cornmeal

1 tablespoon (15 g) fresh herbs (a combination of rosemary, thyme, and oregano or marjoram)

Combine garlic with olive oil and set aside. Mix flour, salt, and stout until sticky dough is formed. Knead with floured hands on a floured surface until smooth and elastic. Let dough rest for 10 minutes; meanwhile, preheat oven to 475°F (240°C, or gas mark 9). Line a baking pan with parchment paper.

On a floured board or marble, roll out dough to a circle or rectangle about ¼-inch (6 mm) thick, whatever shape can be accommodated by your baking sheet. Sprinkle cornmeal over the top of your dough and invert it onto paper so that cornmeal side is on the bottom. Brush the top with the garlic-infused oil and sprinkle with herbs.

Bake 6 to 10 minutes, depending on thickness. Bubbles will form while baking. Serve warm or let cool for use as a base for dips and cheese spread or pizza crust.

Prep = 25 minutes   **Cook** = 6 to 10 minutes
Yield = 1 flatbread; 2 to 4 servings

Rhode Island
Johnnycakes with Beer
and Maple Butter

I used to love to drive out to Westerly,
Rhode Island, to dine at Shelter Harbor Inn, where
the highlight of my meal was the johnnycakes served
with maple butter. Even if it seemed incongruous
with the rest of what we ordered from the dinner
menu, they were part of the tradition. I later
developed my own version, using beer,
which has a slight leavening effect.

1 egg
2 cups (275 g) white or yellow cornmeal
1 teaspoon salt
1 bottle (12 ounces, or 355 ml) beer
Butter, for cooking
Maple butter
Maple syrup, warmed

Beat egg in a medium bowl. Stir in corn meal, salt, and beer. Allow to stand for 15 minutes. Melt a little butter in a large nonstick skillet or on a nonstick griddle. Drop spoonfuls of batter onto the buttered surface and cook to a golden brown on each side, flipping with a spatula. You can cook three or four johnnycakes at a time, adding butter as you go. Stir batter occasionally to keep well mixed. Serve hot with scoops of maple butter and a pitcher of warm maple syrup.

To make maple butter: Whip 1 stick (112 g) unsalted butter, softened, with 3 tablespoons (60 g) maple syrup until fluffy.

Prep = 10 minutes   **Stand** = 15 minutes   **Cook** = 15 to 18 minutes
Yield = 12 johnnycakes; 4 servings

Blueberry
Beer Muffins

Beer adds a yeast bread quality to everyone's breakfast favorite, blueberry muffins. If you don't have fresh fruit, substitute frozen blueberries that have been thawed and drained well.

2 cups (240 g) baking mix, such as Bisquick
2 tablespoons (25 g) sugar
2 teaspoons (10 ml) vanilla extract
6 ounces beer (half of a 12-ounce [335 ml] bottle)
1 cup (145 g) blueberries

Preheat oven to 400°F (200°C, or gas mark 6). Spray twelve muffin cups with nonstick spray or line with baking paper liners. In a medium bowl, combine baking mix, sugar, vanilla, and beer with a wire whisk just until blended. Stir in blueberries. Divide batter evenly among muffin cups.

Bake for 10 to 14 minutes, or until golden brown.

Prep = 10 minutes   **Cook** = 10 to 14 minutes   **Yield** = 12 muffins

Blue Cheese
Beer Muffins

Beer and blue cheese combine to make
a marvelous savory muffin to serve with brunch
or in a basket of dinner rolls.

2 ½ cups (312 g) all-purpose flour
1 ½ tablespoons (18 g) sugar
1 teaspoon caraway seeds
1 teaspoons (4.6 g) baking powder
½ teaspoon salt
½ teaspoon cracked black pepper
1 large egg
¼ cup (55 g) unsalted butter, melted and cooled slightly
2 teaspoons (10 g) Dijon mustard
1 can or bottle (12 ounces, or 355 ml) beer, at room temperature
¾ cup (90 g) shredded sharp Cheddar cheese
½ cup (60 g) crumbled blue cheese

Preheat oven to 400°F (200°C, or gas mark 6). Spray twelve
muffin cups with nonstick spray or line with foil baking liners.
(Paper liners stick to cheese and are difficult to remove.) In a
bowl, whisk flour, sugar, caraway seeds, baking powder, salt, and
pepper together; set aside.

In another bowl, whisk together the egg, melted butter, and
mustard until blended. Gently whisk in the beer until the foaming
subsides, then add the cheese. Finally, stir in the flour mixture with
a wooden spoon until moistened. Fill prepared muffin cups three-
quarters full; bake for 20 minutes or until muffins have lumpy
brown tops and a toothpick comes out almost clean.

Prep = 10 minutes   **Cook** = 20 minutes   **Yield** = 12 muffins

Desserts

Mocha Porter Pie

This is really a coffee-flavored version of good old-fashioned grasshopper pie. The filling is made with melted marshmallows. The trick in making this is to use a wire whisk throughout the whole process, to keep the marshmallows from becoming too gelatinous.

 32 large marshmallows
 ½ cup (120 ml) milk
 ½ cup (120 ml) mocha porter
 1 ½ cups (355 ml) chilled whipping cream
 ½ cup (62 g) chopped toasted almonds

CHOCOLATE CRUST:
 1 ½ cups (150 g) crushed chocolate wafers
 3 tablespoons (42 g) dark brown sugar
 ¼ cup (55 g) butter, melted

In a saucepan, heat marshmallows and milk over medium heat, stirring constantly, just until marshmallows melt. Chill until mixture begins to thicken and blend in mocha porter. In a separate bowl, beat whipping cream until stiff peaks form and gently fold into mocha mixture. Spoon into cooled pie shell and sprinkle with toasted almonds.

To make chocolate crust: Preheat oven to 350°F (180°C, or gas mark 4). Combine crushed chocolate wafers, brown sugar, and butter in a bowl. Press into the bottom and sides of a 9-inch (22.5 cm) pie plate. Bake 6 to 8 minutes and let cool completely.

Note: To toast almonds: Preheat oven to 350°F (180°C, or gas mark 4) and spread almonds on a baking sheet. Bake for 6 to 8 minutes, stirring once or twice, until evenly golden brown. Watch carefully to avoid burning.

Prep = 20 minutes   **Cook** = 16 to 19 minutes   **Yield** = 8 servings

BC's Orange-Ginger Cake with Bock Buttercream

This recipe is an adaptation of one that was passed along to me from my Aunt BC in North Carolina. If you don't have any bock beer around the house, a strong stout or porter will give the cake a similar character.

1 box (14.5 ounces, or 411 g) gingerbread mix
1 large egg
1 bottle (12 ounces, or 355 ml) bock beer
1 tablespoon (16 g) grated orange zest
⅓ cup (55 g) golden raisins
½ cup (62 g) toasted almonds (see Note)

BOCK BUTTERCREAM:
⅓ cup (75 g) butter, softened
3 cups (300 g) confectioners' sugar
1 teaspoon vanilla extract
1 teaspoon grated orange zest
3 tablespoons (42 ml) bock beer

Preheat oven to 350°F (180°C, or gas mark 4). Combine gingerbread mix, egg, beer, orange zest, and raisins in a bowl just until moistened and blended (do not overmix). Pour into an 8-inch (20 cm) square baking pan lined with parchment paper. Bake for 35 minutes, or until a toothpick inserted in the center comes out clean. Let cool for 10 minutes in the pan, then invert on a wire rack and let cool completely. Peel off parchment from the bottom of the cake.

For the bock buttercream: Beat together all ingredients in a bowl. Frost the top and sides of the cake with bock buttercream and sprinkle with toasted almonds.

Note: To toast almonds: Preheat oven to 350°F (180°C, or gas mark 4) and spread almonds on a baking sheet. Bake for 6 to 8 minutes, stirring once or twice, until evenly golden brown. Watch carefully to avoid burning.

Prep = 18 minutes   **Cook** = 35 minutes
Yield = 8 to 12 servings

Apple Fritters in Beer Batter with Cider Sauce

These irresistible little fruit-filled doughnuts
are really worth the effort for a melt-in-your-mouth
dessert. If you skip the ice cream, they make
a great brunch or breakfast treat.

¾ cup (94 g) all-purpose flour

¼ teaspoon salt

2 eggs, separated

2 tablespoons (30 ml) vegetable oil, plus extra for deep-frying

¼ cup (60 ml) flat beer

2 or 3 apples, peeled, cored, and sliced into ¾-inch
(1.8 cm) thick rings

Vanilla or cinnamon ice cream

CIDER SAUCE:

¼ cup (55 g) butter

¼ cup (85 g) corn syrup

1 cup (225 g) dark brown sugar, firmly packed

½ teaspoon ground cinnamon

¼ teaspoon grated nutmeg

¼ cup (71 g) frozen apple juice concentrate, thawed

¼ cup (60 ml) heavy cream

In a bowl, combine flour, salt, and egg yolks and blend in oil with a whisk. Blend in beer. Chill batter for 30 minutes. Beat egg whites in separate bowl until soft peaks form and gently fold into chilled batter with a wire whisk. Preheat oil in a deep fryer to 375°F (190°C, or gas mark 5). Dip apples into batter and fry one or two at a time until golden, turning once. Drain on paper towels. Serve warm with cider sauce and scoops of ice cream.

For cider sauce: Combine ingredients in a medium saucepan and bring to a boil. Reduce heat and simmer for 3 to 5 minutes. Serve warm.

Prep = 20 minutes   **Chill** = 30 minutes
Cook = 20 minutes   **Yield** = 4 servings

Apricot Ale Cheesecake

Fruit-flavored beers have become trendy in the craft beer market. This crustless apricot cheesecake features apricot beer and dried apricots.

2 packages (8 ounces, or 115 g, each) cream cheese, softened

½ cup (100 g) sugar

2 tablespoons (16 g) flour

4 eggs

¼ cup (55 g) unsalted butter, melted and cooled

Finely grated zest of 1 lemon

1 cup (235 ml) apricot-flavored beer

½ cup (65 g) chopped dried apricots

In a large bowl, beat cream cheese. Add the sugar and beat until blended. Beat in the flour and the eggs, one at a time. Beat in butter, lemon zest, and apricot beer. Stir in chopped apricots.

Preheat oven to 350°F (180°C, or gas mark 4) and grease an 8-inch (20 cm) diameter, 3-inch (7.5 cm) deep springform pan. Pour mixture into prepared pan and bake on the middle rack of oven for 1½ hours. Transfer to a cake rack to cool. Chill for at least 3 hours before serving.

Prep = 15 minutes   **Chill** = 3 hours
Cook = 1½ hours   **Yield** = 10 servings

Irish Pumpkin Pie with Guinness and Golden Raisins

The next time you are serving a traditional fall holiday dinner, try baking this Irish pumpkin pie! The stout and golden raisins are a great change of pace from that obligatory recipe on the back of the canned pumpkin.

¼ cup (55 g) butter
1 cup (150 g) light brown sugar
1 teaspoon ground cinnamon
½ teaspoon ground ginger
¼ teaspoon grated nutmeg
½ teaspoon salt
1 ¾ cups (430 g) canned solid-pack pumpkin
6 ounces (half of a 12-ounce [355 ml] bottle) Guinness Stout
2 eggs
½ cup (82 g) golden raisins, packed
9-inch (22.5 cm) unbaked pie shell

Preheat over to 425°F (220°C, or gas mark 7). Melt butter in a medium saucepan over low heat. Blend in brown sugar, cinnamon, ginger, nutmeg, and salt. Blend in pumpkin, stout, and eggs, with a wire whisk until smooth. Stir in raisins and pour mixture into pie shell. Place on a baking sheet on the bottom oven rack. Bake for 15 minutes at 425°F (220°C, or gas mark 7). Reduce heat to 350°F (180°C, or gas mark 4) and bake for an additional 45 to 50 minutes, or until a fork placed in center of the pie comes out clean. Let cool on rack 2 hours before serving.

Prep = 20 minutes   **Cool** = 2 hours
Cook = 1 hour to 1 hour 5 minutes   **Yield** = 8 servings

Banana Beignets
with Praline Ice Cream
and Rum Sauce

Years ago, I used to order a similar dessert
at the Tavern on the Green in New York City's
Central Park. Their banana fritters were served with
a chocolate sauce. I later devised a recipe using a
sauce similar to bananas Foster and changed the
name from banana fritters to banana beignets.

    2 cups (250 g) sifted all-purpose flour
    1 packet (¼ ounce, or 7 g) dry active yeast
    1 teaspoon kosher salt
    ¼ cup plus 1 tablespoon (62 g) sugar
    1 teaspoon ground cinnamon
    ¼ cup (60 ml) canola oil
    2 eggs, separated, plus one egg white
 1 ¼ cups (285 ml) cold, light beer
    3 large bananas
      Confectioners' sugar
      Praline ice cream

BANANA RUM SAUCE:
    ¼ cup (55 g) butter
    1 cup (225 g) dark brown sugar, firmly packed
    ¼ teaspoon ground cinnamon
    ¼ cup (82 g) light corn syrup
    ¼ cup (60 ml) banana rum
    ¼ cup (60 ml) heavy cream

In a large bowl, stir together flour, yeast, salt, ¼ cup (50 g) of sugar, and cinnamon. In another bowl, combine canola oil, egg yolks, and beer. Combine the dry and wet ingredients and blend with a wire whisk until all the lumps are gone.

In a separate bowl with electric mixer, beat egg whites with the remaining tablespoon (12 g) of sugar to medium-soft peak stage. Carefully fold the egg whites into the beer batter. Cover batter and let rest at room temperature for 1 hour.

Preheat a deep fryer to 375°F (190°C). Peel bananas, cut in half, and then slice lengthwise. Dip in batter and deep-fry, a few pieces at a time, until golden brown and crispy. Drain on paper towels and dust with confectioners' sugar. Arrange two pieces of bananas each on six dessert plates. Serve with scoops of praline ice cream, centered between bananas, and drizzle with banana rum sauce.

For banana rum sauce: In a medium saucepan, melt butter and stir in brown sugar, cinnamon, corn syrup, banana rum, and heavy cream. Bring to a boil, reduce heat, and simmer for 1 minute. Remove from heat and let cool to lukewarm.

Prep = 20 minutes **Stand** = 1 hour **Cook** = 18 minutes
Yield = 6 servings

Stout and Sauerkraut Fudge Cake

This is one of those recipes that is even wackier than tomato soup cake. Once upon a time, carrot cake was a novelty, but now it has been a mainstream dessert for decades. Sauerkraut in chocolate cake may not have yet caught on, but it is a sure hit with anyone who tries it. The almond extract gives it the flavor of macaroons, while the sauerkraut mimics the texture of coconut.

⅓ cup (55 g) butter, softened
⅓ cup (55 g) shortening
1 ½ cups (300 g) sugar
3 eggs
1 teaspoon almond extract
½ cup (43 g) unsweetened cocoa powder
2 ½ cups (312 g) all-purpose flour
1 teaspoon baking soda
1 teaspoon baking powder
¼ teaspoon salt
1 cup (235 ml) beer
⅔ cup (150 g) sauerkraut, rinsed, drained, and chopped

CHOCOLATE-CREAM CHEESE FROSTING:
8 ounces (225 g) semisweet chocolate
6 ounces (170 g) cream cheese, softened
2 cups (200 g) confectioners' sugar
¼ teaspoon salt
1 teaspoon almond extract
2 to 3 tablespoons (28 to 42 ml) light cream
⅓ cup (42 g) sliced, toasted almonds

Preheat oven to 350°F (180°C, or gas mark 4) and grease and flour a Bundt pan. Cream butter, shortening, and sugar in bowl until light and fluffy. Beat in eggs and almond extract. Sift together cocoa, flour, baking soda, baking powder, and salt. Add dry ingredients alternately with beer to creamed ingredients, starting and ending with dry ingredients. Stir in chopped sauerkraut. Pour into prepared pan. Bake for 50 to 60 minutes.

To make frosting: Melt chocolate in top of double boiler over hot, not boiling water. In a separate bowl, beat melted chocolate into cream cheese. Blend in confectioners' sugar, salt, almond extract, and cream until a spreading consistency. Frost top and sides of cake. Sprinkle with almonds.

Note: To toast almonds: Preheat oven to 350°F (180°C, or gas mark 4) and spread almonds on a baking sheet. Bake for 6 to 8 minutes, stirring once or twice, until evenly golden brown. Watch carefully to avoid burning.

Prep = 35 minutes   **Cook** = 1 hour to 1 hour 10 minutes
Yield = 12 servings

Chocolate Bock Beeramisu

This version of tiramisu is equally good with a chocolate- or a mocha-flavored porter.

  6 large egg yolks
  ¾ cup (150 g) sugar
  ⅔ cup (175 ml) milk
  1 teaspoon instant espresso powder
  1 pound (455 g) mascarpone cheese
  ⅔ cup (156 ml) Samuel Adams Chocolate Bock
  1 tablespoon (14 g) brown sugar, firmly packed
  2 packages (3 ounces, or 85 g, each) ladyfingers
1 ¼ cups (355 ml) whipping cream, whipped to stiff peaks
     Unsweetened cocoa powder

In a medium saucepan, beat egg yolks and sugar with a wire whisk, then blend in milk and instant espresso. Heat to boiling over medium heat, stirring constantly; reduce heat to low. Boil and stir for 1 minute, then remove from heat. Pour into a medium bowl and place plastic wrap directly onto the surface of the custard mixture. Refrigerate for at least 2 hours, until chilled.

Blend mascarpone cheese into custard with an electric mixer. In a separate bowl, combine beer and brown sugar. Separate ladyfingers and brush cut side with espresso mixture. Arrange half of ladyfingers, cut side up, in a 7 × 11-inch (15.5 × 27.5 cm) glass baking dish. Spread half of cheese mixture over ladyfingers, followed by half of whipped cream. Repeat layers with remaining ladyfingers, cheese mixture, and whipped cream. Sprinkle with cocoa powder.

Refrigerate for at least 4 hours before serving but not longer than 24 hours.

Prep = 20 minute   **Cook** = 6 minutes
Chill = 2 hours, plus at least 4 hours   **Yield** = 8 servings

Honey-Almond Beer Cake

This dense spice cake is reminiscent
of a fruitcake. Try adding this version
to your holiday gift-giving list.

- ½ cup (112 g) butter
- 2 cups (400 g) sugar
- 4 eggs
- ½ cup (120 ml) orange juice
- ½ cup (140 g) apple butter
- ¾ cup (255 g) honey
- 1 teaspoon almond extract
- 4 cups (500 g) sifted all-purpose flour
- 2 teaspoons (9.2 g) baking powder
- ¼ teaspoon salt
- 1 teaspoon baking soda
- 1 teaspoon grated nutmeg
- 1 teaspoon ground cloves
- 1 teaspoon ground cinnamon
- 1 teaspoon ground allspice
- ½ cup (62 g) chopped toasted slivered almonds
- 1 cup (145 g) golden raisins
- 1 cup (235 ml) beer
- Confectioners' sugar

Preheat oven to 325°F (170°C, or gas mark 3). Grease and flour a
tube pan. Cream butter and sugar in medium bowl until fluffy. Add
eggs, one at a time, beating well after each addition. Add orange
juice, apple butter, honey, and almond extract. Mix well. In a separate
bowl, sift flour together with baking powder, salt, baking soda, and
spices. Toss 2 tablespoons (28 g) of flour mixture with almonds and
raisins. Add rest of flour mixture to butter mixture alternately with
beer, beginning and ending with flour mixture. Add raisin-almond
mixture and stir. Pour batter into prepared pan. Bake for 1 hour and
20 minutes. Let cool for 10 minutes. Invert pan and remove cake.
Sprinkle top and sides with confectioners' sugar.

Note: To toast almonds: Preheat oven to 350°F (180°C, or gas mark
4) and spread almonds on a baking sheet. Bake for 6 to 8 minutes,
stirring once or twice, until evenly golden brown. Watch carefully to
avoid burning.

Prep = 25 minutes   **Cook** = 1 hour 20 minutes   **Yield** = 12 servings

Mango-Malt Mousse Pie

Fruit-flavored malt beverages, a popular beer alternative, are really versatile when it comes to cooking. This passion fruit–mango pie is a refreshing dessert that you can even make ahead and freeze; defrost slowly in the refrigerator before serving. Please note that this pie contains uncooked egg whites.

1 package (.25 ounce, or 7 g) unflavored gelatin
¼ cup (60 ml) cold water
1 bottle (12 ounces, or 355 ml) passion fruit and mango–flavored malt beverage
½ cup (100 g) sugar, divided
2 eggs, separated
1 teaspoon vanilla extract
1 cup (235 ml) heavy cream, whipped
Toasted coconut

GRAHAM CRACKER CRUST:
1 ½ cups (150 g) crushed graham cracker crumbs
3 tablespoons (37 g) sugar
⅓ cup (75 g) butter, melted

Soften gelatin in cold water for 5 minutes. In the top part of a double boiler over simmering water, combine malt beverage and 6 tablespoons (75 g) sugar. Stir until dissolved. Whisk in egg yolks and cook in double boiler until thickened, stirring constantly. Stir gelatin into custard mixture until thoroughly dissolved. Cool mixture over a bowl of ice water, stirring just until it starts to mound from a spoon but has not set.

In a medium bowl, whip egg whites and vanilla until frothy. Gradually add remaining sugar, one teaspoon at a time, beating constantly until whites form soft peaks. Fold meringue into custard, along with whipped cream. Spoon mixture into graham cracker crust. Sprinkle with toasted coconut and chill for at least 4 hours or until set.

To make graham cracker crust: Combine graham cracker crumbs with sugar in a bowl. Stir in melted butter. Preheat oven to 350°F (180°C, or gas mark 4). Press crumbs into 9-inch (22.5 cm) pie plate and bake for 8 minutes. Let cool completely before filling.

Prep = 35 minutes   **Cook** = 25 minutes   **Chill** = 4 hours

Hard Lime Pie

Whoever first coined the expression "easy as pie" must have been referring to frozen key lime pie. For a contemporary adult version, I've used a lime-flavored malt beverage.

1 can (14 ounces, or 425 ml) sweetened condensed milk
⅓ cup (78 ml) Mike's hard lime beverage
3 tablespoons (52 g) frozen limeade concentrate, thawed
1 teaspoon grated lime peel
    Green food coloring (if desired)
1 container (10 ounces, or 280 g) frozen whipped topping, thawed

GRAHAM CRACKER CRUST:
1 ½ cups (150 g) crushed graham cracker crumbs
3 tablespoons (37 g) sugar
⅓ cup (75 g) butter, melted

Combine sweetened condensed milk with hard lime beverage, limeade concentrate, and lime peel in a bowl. Blend with a wire whisk. Gently fold in whipped topping and spoon into the graham cracker crust. Freeze for at least 4 hours, or until firm.

To make cracker crust: Combine crushed graham cracker crumbs with sugar in a bowl. Stir in melted butter. Preheat oven to 350°F (180°C, or gas mark 4). Press crumbs into 9-inch (22.5 cm) pie plate and bake for 8 minutes. Let cool completely before filling.

Prep = 20 minutes   **Cook** = 8 minutes
Freeze = 4 hours   **Yield** = 8 servings

Hard Lemonade Cake

This is one of those simple,
shortcut recipes in which mixes work magic.
I first created this recipe for a neighborhood
restaurant, the Black Rock Castle. The owner liked
it so much, she wanted to send one
to her mother in Ireland.

1 box (18.25 ounces, or 525 g) lemon cake mix

1 cup (235 ml) water

1 bottle (12 ounces, or 355 ml) hard lemonade, divided

⅓ cup (78 ml) cooking oil

3 large eggs

1 can (12 ounces, or 340 g) frozen lemonade concentrate, thawed

4 ounces (half of 8-ounce [225 g] package) cream cheese, softened

2 pints (950 ml) whipping cream

1 box (3 ounces, or 85 g) instant lemon pudding mix

½ cup (62 g) chopped toasted almonds

Preheat oven to 350°F (180°C, or gas mark 4). Lightly grease and flour a 9 × 13-inch (22.5 × 32.5 cm) sheet cake pan. Combine cake mix, water, ⅓ cup (78 ml) of hard lemonade, oil, and eggs in a large bowl and beat with electric mixer at low speed for about 30 seconds, until moistened. Scrape down bowl and beat for 2 minutes at medium speed. Pour into pan and bake for 32 to 35 minutes, or until a toothpick inserted in the center comes out clean. Let cool completely.

Combine remaining hard lemonade with lemonade concentrate. Reserving ½ cup (120 ml) of mixture, pierce cake with a fork and pour the remaining lemonade mixture evenly over cake, allowing it to seep in. In a large bowl, beat cream cheese until smooth and slowly beat in reserved ⅓ cup (78 ml) of lemonade mixture. Add cream and pudding mix. Beat on medium-high speed until stiff peaks form and spread over cake. Sprinkle with toasted almonds and chill until serving time.

Note: To toast almonds: Preheat oven to 350°F (180°C, or gas mark 4) and spread almonds on a baking sheet. Bake for 6 to 8 minutes, stirring once or twice, until evenly golden brown. Watch carefully to avoid burning.

Prep = 20 minutes   **Cook** = 32 to 35 minutes   **Yield** = 12 servings

Porter-Roasted Pears with Macaroon Crumbs

This is a simple dessert and a light finish
to any meal. When coring the pears, remove center
seeds with a melon baller, leaving an impression
for the mascarpone cheese filling.

4 firm, ripe Bartlett pears, unpeeled, halved lengthwise and cored
2 tablespoons (30 ml) lemon juice
2 tablespoons (24 g) sugar
⅓ cup (78 ml) porter
1 cup (120 g) mascarpone cheese
8 amaretti cookies, crushed

Preheat oven to 375°F (190°C, or gas mark 5). Coat pears with lemon juice and sugar and place cut side down in a 9 × 13-inch (22.5 × 32.5 cm) baking pan. Pour beer over pears and cover tightly with aluminum foil. Bake for 25 to 30 minutes, or until pears are easily pierced with a toothpick. Place each cut side up on a serving plate. Top each with 2 tablespoons (15 g) of cheese and one crumbled cookie. Drizzle with pan juices.

Prep = 10 minutes   **Cook** = 25 to 30 minutes   **Yield** = 8 servings

Tropical Fruit Trifle

Tropical fruit flavored malts make island-inspired desserts. Using frozen pineapple minimizes the amount of liquid released into the trifle. Fresh frozen pineapple chunks or even well-drained canned fruit can be used as well.

PINEAPPLE PASTRY CREAM:

- 2 packages (3.3 ounces, or 94 g, each) vanilla pudding mix (regular, not instant)
- 3 ½ cups (830 ml) half-and-half
- ½ cup (120 ml) from 12-ounce (355 ml) bottle pineapple colada malt-flavored beverage
- 6 tablespoons (83 g) butter

WHIPPED CREAM MIXTURE:

- 1 pint (475 ml) whipping cream
- ¼ cup (57 g) sour cream
- ⅓ cup (33 g) confectioners' sugar
- ½ teaspoon coconut extract

TO ASSEMBLE:

- 1 (10- to 12-ounce, or 280 to 340 g) pound cake
- 1 cup (235 ml) from 12-ounce (355 ml) bottle pineapple colada malt-flavored beverage
- 1 jar (12 ounces, or 340 g) pineapple jam
- 3 cups (450 g) frozen pineapple chunks, thawed and well drained
- 3 kiwi fruit, peeled and sliced
- ⅓ cup (23 g) shredded coconut

For pastry cream: Prepare pudding mix according to package directions, substituting half-and-half and pineapple colada malt-flavored beverage for milk. Once thickened, remove from heat and whisk in butter until melted and smooth. Transfer to a bowl and press plastic wrap over the surface of cream. Chill for at least 4 hours.

For whipped cream mixture: Combine whipping cream, sour cream, confectioners' sugar, and coconut extract in a large bowl and beat until stiff but not dry peaks form. Set aside.

To assemble: Slice pound cake into twelve slices and then cut each slice into six cubes. Arrange one-third of pound cake in the bottom of a trifle bowl or large soufflé dish. Using a pastry brush, brush cubes with pineapple colada malt-flavored beverage. Stir up jam and spread over cake cubes. Top with one-third of pineapple followed by one-third of pastry cream and one-third of whipped cream mixture. Repeat layering, ending with whipped cream mixture, and garnish with kiwi slices. Sprinkle with coconut. Cover with plastic wrap and refrigerate for 3 hours before serving but not longer than 24 hours.

Prep = 40 minutes   **Cook** = 10 minutes   **Chill** = 7 hours
Yield = 12 servings

Peanut Brittle Praline Beer Puffs

Years ago while in college, I had a radio show called Alison's Restaurant. Part of my hosting the show was preparing a gourmet "goodie gift" for my guest. When I had the honor of interviewing Julia Child, I presented these peanut brittle puffs as an American version of profiteroles. Soon after the show, I got a postcard from the Hotel Dorset in New York City, thanking me for the "great invention."

1 cup (235 ml) beer

½ cup (112 g) butter

1 cup (125 g) all-purpose flour

¼ teaspoon salt

4 eggs

⅓ cup (78 g) crushed peanut brittle for topping

PEANUT BRITTLE CREAM:

1 pint (475 ml) whipping cream

1 tablespoon (14 g) brown sugar

½ package (3.3 ounce, or 94 g) instant vanilla pudding mix

⅓ cup (78 g) crushed peanut brittle

CHOCOLATE GLAZE:

2 ounces (28 g) unsweetened chocolate

2 tablespoons (28 g) butter

1 teaspoon vanilla extract

2 cups (200 g) confectioners' sugar

¼ cup (60 ml) hot water

Preheat oven to 450°F (230°C, or gas mark 8). Line a large baking sheet with parchment paper. In a heavy saucepan, heat beer and butter until it barely comes to a boil and the butter is melted. Using a wire whisk, add flour and salt, lower heat, and stir constantly until the mixture pulls away from the side of the pan and forms a ball. Remove from the heat and let rest for 1 minute. Add eggs, beating in one at a time, each time until the dough is shiny. Drop by spoonfuls or pipe dough in twelve 1-inch (2.5 cm) mounds onto prepared baking sheet. Bake for 10 minutes at 450°F (230°C, or gas mark 8). Reduce heat to 350°F (180°C, or gas mark 4). Bake for an additional 10 minutes, until brown and dry. Let cool away from moisture.

Split beer puffs and use a pastry bag to fill them with peanut brittle cream. Top with glaze and sprinkle with crushed peanut brittle.

For peanut brittle cream: Beat whipping cream with brown sugar and the half package of vanilla instant pudding mix. Fold in crushed peanut brittle.

Chocolate glaze: Melt unsweetened chocolate with butter and vanilla. Remove from heat and blend in confectioners' sugar and hot water until smooth.

Prep = 30 minutes   **Cook** = 25 to 30 minutes   **Yield** = 6 servings

Peanut Butter and Porter Pie

Peanut butter cup lovers, this recipe is for you. The filling is generous, so I use a 9-inch (22.5 cm) springform pan instead of a pie pan to prevent it from running over the sides. This recipe will also fill two 6-ounce (170 g) prepared graham cracker pie shells.

1 package (8 ounces, or 225 g) cream cheese
½ cup (115 g) brown sugar, packed
⅔ cup (172 g) peanut butter
¼ cup (60 ml) half-and-half
⅓ cup (80 ml) porter
1 tub (8 ounces, or 225 g) frozen whipped topping, thawed
½ cup (63 g) roasted, unsalted peanuts, chopped

PEANUT BUTTER GRAHAM CRACKER CRUST:
3 tablespoons (37 g) sugar
1 ½ cups (150 g) crushed graham crackers
¼ cup (55 g) butter
¼ cup (63 g) peanut butter

In a bowl with an electric mixer, beat together cream cheese, brown sugar, and peanut butter until blended. Slowly blend in half-and-half and porter. Beat until smooth. Fold in whipped topping. Spoon into prepared crust. Sprinkle with peanuts and freeze until firm.

For crust: Preheat oven to 350°F (180°C, or gas mark 4). Combine sugar and graham cracker crumbs in a mixing bowl . Melt butter and peanut butter together in a small saucepan over low heat. Stir into graham cracker crumbs. Press mixture into the bottom and sides of a 9-inch (22.5 cm) pie plate. Bake for 8 minutes.

Prep = 20 minutes   **Cook** = 5 minutes   **Yield** = 8 to 10 servings

Lambic Pêche Grilled Peaches and Cream

Lambic Pêche (peach) is a great dessert beer and very useful for macerating fresh fruit. In this recipe, fresh peaches are soaked in it, grilled, and topped with an almond-flavored cream.

6 large fresh, freestone peaches, halved and pitted
1 bottle (12 ounces, or 355 ml) Lambic Pêche, divided
1 cup (328 g) caramel sauce
2 packages (3 ounces, or 85 g, each) cream cheese, softened
¼ teaspoon almond extract
½ cup (50 g) confectioners' sugar
1 cup (235 ml) whipping cream
  Granulated sugar
  Toasted chopped almonds (see Note)

Place peaches in a baking dish, cut side down, in 1 cup (235 ml) of Lambic Pêche. Cover with plastic wrap and chill for about 3 hours. Heat remaining ¼ cup (120 ml) of beer with caramel sauce until blended. Remove from heat and let stand until it reaches room temperature. With electric mixer, beat cream cheese, almond extract, and confectioners' sugar in a bowl until smooth and fluffy. Blend in cream and beat until stiff peaks form. Chill in the refrigerator until ready to serve.

Preheat a lightly oiled grill to medium-high. Remove peaches from beer and pat dry. Dip cut sides in granulated sugar and place cut side down on grill. Grill for 5 minutes, or until grill marks appear on cooked surface of peaches, Place two halves, cut side up, on each of six dessert plates. Drizzle with beer-caramel mixture and top with cheese-cream mixture. Garnish with toasted almonds.

Note: To toast almonds: Preheat oven to 350°F (180°C, or gas mark 4) and spread almonds on a baking sheet. Bake for 6 to 8 minutes, stirring once or twice, until evenly golden brown. Watch carefully to avoid burning.

Prep = 15 minutes   **Chill** = 3 hours
Cook = 5 minutes   **Yield** = 6 servings

Pineapple-Pecan Beer Bread Pudding with Brown Sugar–Beer Sauce

If you like pineapple upside-down cake, you'll love this bread pudding with pineapple, pecans, and a brown sugar–beer sauce. For best results, drain as much liquid as possible from the pineapple.

1 can (12 ounces, or 355 ml) beer

1 cup (235 ml) half-and-half

½ cup (120 ml) heavy cream

4 eggs

½ cup (115 g) brown sugar, firmly packed

¼ teaspoon ground cinnamon

1 teaspoon vanilla extract

1 can (16 ounces, or 455 g) crushed pineapple, very well drained (press in colander)

4 cups (360 g) dried white bread cubes

½ cup (50 g) chopped pecans

BROWN SUGAR–BEER SAUCE:

¼ cup (55 g) butter

1 cup (225 g) brown sugar, firmly packed

¼ cup (85 g) light corn syrup

¼ cup (60 ml) beer

1 teaspoon vanilla extract

½ cup (120 ml) heavy cream

In a large bowl, combine beer, half-and-half, heavy cream, and eggs. Blend in brown sugar, cinnamon, vanilla, and pineapple. Gently stir in bread cubes and pour into a 2-quart (2 L) buttered casserole. Cover with plastic wrap and chill for at least 2 hours.

Preheat oven to 325°F (170°C, or gas mark 3). Sprinkle bread pudding with pecans. Bake for 50 minutes, or until a knife inserted in the center comes out clean. Serve warm with brown sugar–beer sauce.

For sauce: Combine butter, brown sugar, corn syrup, beer, vanilla, and heavy cream. Bring to a boil, reduce heat, and simmer for about 3 minutes.

Prep = 20 minutes   **Chill** = 2 hours
Cook = 50 minutes to 1 hour   **Yield** = 8 servings

Poached Pears
in Lambic Framboise

Poaching pears in beer is really just a new spin
on the classic pears poached in wine. Belgian lambic
beers come in a wonderful array of fruity flavors;
framboise is particularly good in this recipe.

> 6 fresh pears
> ½ cup (120 ml) Lambic Framboise
> ¼ cup (50 g) sugar
> 1 package (10 ounces, or 280 g) frozen raspberries, thawed

Preheat oven to 350°F (180°C, or gas mark 4). Pare pears, leaving
stems intact. Arrange pears in a 2-quart (2 L) casserole. Combine
Lambic Framboise and sugar, and pour over pears. Cover casserole
and bake until pears are tender when pierced with a fork, 45 to 50
minutes.

Meanwhile, press raspberries through a sieve so that you have a
pulpy syrup (discard seeds in sieve). Drain liquid off the poached
pears, turning to coat. Pour raspberry syrup over pears, cover, and
refrigerate for 12 hours, turning three or four times to allow raspberry syrup to evenly macerate pears. To serve, arrange pears
upright in dessert dishes and spoon raspberry syrup over each.

Prep = 20 minutes   **Cook** = 45 to 50 minutes
Chill = 12 hours   **Yield** = 6 servings

Stout Ice Cream–Praline Sundae

Brown sugar and stout give this homemade
ice cream a rich, caramel flavor. When topped with
praline sauce and glazed pecans, it becomes an
exquisite frozen confection. For candied pecans,
use commercially packaged ones
or experiment with homemade.

1 bottle (12 ounces, or 355 ml) Guinness Stout
2 cups (475 ml) half-and-half
¾ cup (168 g) dark brown sugar, firmly packed
2 teaspoons (10 ml) vanilla extract
6 egg yolks
Sugar-glazed pecans

GUINNESS PRALINE SAUCE:
1 cup (225 g) dark brown sugar, firmly packed
½ cup (112 g) butter
¼ cup (85 g) corn syrup
¼ cup (60 ml) heavy cream
¼ cup (60 ml) Guinness stout

Combine the stout, half-and-half, milk, brown sugar, and vanilla in a medium, heavy saucepan. Bring to a gentle boil over medium heat. Remove from the heat. Beat the egg yolks in a medium bowl. Whisk 1 cup (235 ml) of the hot stout mixture into the egg yolks. Gradually add the egg mixture in a slow, steady stream, to the hot cream. Cook over medium-low heat, stirring occasionally, until the mixture thickens enough to coat the back of a spoon or reaches 170°F (77°C), about 5 minutes. Remove from the heat and strain through a fine-mesh strainer into a clean container. Cover with plastic wrap, pressing down against the surface to keep a skin from forming. Chill in the refrigerator for 2 hours.

Remove from refrigerator and add the stout mixture, whisking until well blended. Pour into the bowl of an ice-cream machine and freeze according to the manufacturer's instructions. Transfer to an airtight container and freeze. Serve in scoops topped with Guinness praline sauce and candied pecans.

For Guinness praline sauce: Combine brown sugar, butter, corn syrup, cream, and stout in a heavy-bottomed medium saucepan and bring to a boil. Cook, stirring constantly, for 2 minutes. Remove from heat and let cool slightly before serving.

Note: This sauce maybe be kept in a jar in the refrigerator and reheated as needed.

Prep = 20 minutes   **Cook** = 15 minutes
Chill = 2 hours   **Yield** = 6 to 8 servings

Raspberry-Root Beer Torte

At first, this cake seems quirky, but root beer has
a unique blend of spices that works well with layers
of raspberry jam and root beer–laced cream.

4 eggs
1 package (18.25 ounces, or 525 g) yellow cake mix
1 package (3.3 ounces, or 94 g) instant vanilla pudding
1 cup (235 ml) root beer
⅓ cup (78 ml) vegetable oil
1 cup (320 g) raspberry jam

ROOT BEER CREAM:
2 cups (475 ml) heavy cream
1 package (3.3 ounces, or 94 g) instant white chocolate-flavored
pudding mix
⅓ cup (78 ml) root beer

Preheat oven to 350°F (180°C, or gas mark 4). Beat eggs, cake mix,
pudding mix, root beer, and oil in a large bowl for 3 minutes on at
speed. Pour into two 9-inch (22.5 cm) round cake pans lined with
parchment paper. Bake for 28 to 38 minutes, or until cake tests
done in center. Let cool for 10 minutes. Remove from pan and let
cool thoroughly on rack, then remove baking parchment. Split layers
in half horizontally and fill with raspberry jam. Stack together with
root beer cream and use it to frost sides and top.

For root beer cream: Combine heavy cream, pudding mix, and root
beer in a large bowl. Beat at high speed until stiff peaks form.

Prep = 20 minutes   **Cook** = 28 to 38 minutes   **Yield** = 12 servings

Index

appetizers
  Baby Beer Burger Bites, 20
  Beer Cheese Spread, 23
  Buffalo Beer Wings, 29
  Chiles con Queso Reduction, 33
  Drunken Beer Dogs, 22
  Lambic Hot Crab Dip, 32
  Pepperoni Pizza and Beer Dip,
    28
  Portobello Mushroom Caps with
    Porter-Caramelized Onions,
    26
  Stout and Stilton Pâté, 19
  Swiss-Style Beer Cheese Fondue,
    30
  Thai Chicken Wings with Peanut
    Sauce, 24
BBQ Rub, 112
beans
  Beerbecue Baked Beans, 158
  Chicken Chili with Beer and
    Black Beans, 40
  Green Bean and Portobello
    Mushroom Casserole with
    Porter, 179
  Green Beans with Portobello
    Mushrooms and Porter, 185
beef
  All-American Beer Meat Loaf, 82
  Asian Beer London Broil, 84
  Baby Beer Burger Bites, 20
  Beef, Broccoli, and Beer Stir Fry,
    79
  Beer and Bacon Bolognese
    Sauce, 66
  Beer Beef Stroganoff, 92
  Biergarten Sauerbraten, 89
  Bock-Braised Brisket, 88
  Buffalo-Style Beer and Beef
    Tacos, 90
  Chuck Wagon Beerbecue Roll,
    165
  Filets Mignons Beernaise, 91
  Pilsner Shepherd's Pie, 98
  Skillet Steaks with Porter and
    Peppercorn Sauce, 103

Sloppy Drunk Joes, 104
Smokey Brew Oven-Baked Beer
  Brisket, 170
Steak and Stout Pie, 105
Steak and Stout Stew, 48
beer
  brewing, 6-8
  cooking with, 16-17
  home brewing, 9
  microbrewing, 15
  types of, 9-14
  beer batter, 138, 142, 145, 146,
    173, 177, 178
breads
  Banana Beer Bread, 204
  Beer, Bacon, and Cheddar Corn
    Bread, 208
  Beer Bread Sticks, 206
  Beer Rye Bread, 210
  Blue Cheese Beer Muffins, 217
  Blueberry Beer Muffins, 216
  Classic Beer Biscuits, 212
  Easy Beer Batter Bread, 211
  Flower Pot Porter Pecan Bread,
    207
  Rhode Island Johnnycakes with
    Beer and Maple Butter, 215
  Stout Garlic and Herb Flatbread,
    214
  Sun-Dried Tomato, Olive, and
    Basil Beer Bread, 203
brunch
  Bacon, Tomato, Beer, and Cheese
    Brunch Pie, 187
  Beer, Cheese, and Chive Soufflé,
    193
  Beer and Sausage Strata, 192
  Blueberry-Buckwheat Beer
    Pancakes, 196
  Bourbon Street Brunch Eggs
    with Beer, 200-201
  California Monterey Jack Rabbit,
    197
  Chocolate Bock French Toast,
    190

Classic Welsh Rabbit, 198
Eggs Beeradict, 188
Irish Rabbit, 191
Stout and Sweet Potato Waffles, 194

cheese
Bacon, Tomato, Beer, and Cheese Brunch Pie, 187
Beer, Cheese, and Chive Soufflé, 193
Beer Cheese Spread, 23
Blue Cheese Beer Muffins, 217
California Monterey Jack Rabbit, 197
Classic Welsh Rabbit, 198
Game Day Beer Cheese Soup, 47
Irish Rabbit, 191
Macaroni and Beer Cheese with Bacon, 68
Stout and Stilton Pâté, 19
Swiss-Style Beer Cheese Fondue, 30

chicken
American Classic Beer-Can Chicken, 112
Apple Ale-Honey Mustard Chicken Drumsticks, 110
Apple and Brown Ale-Glazed Chicken, 133
Artichoke Chicken Thighs in Beer, 111
Asian Beer-Chicken Soup, 38
Buffalo Beer Wings, 29
Bulgur Salad with Beer, 50
Caribbean Slow-Cooked Chicken, 114
Carolina-Style Beerbecued Chicken, 162
Chicken Beerkabobs, 116
Chicken Chili with Beer and Black Beans, 40
Coq au Lager, 118
Corn Bread-Crusted Chicken Pot Pie with Pilsner and Artichokes, 120-121
Country-Fried Chicken with Beer Gravy, 122
Hard Lemonade-Grilled Chicken, 126
Henry's Balsamic-Beer Chicken, 127

India Pale Ale British Chicken Curry, 129
Lee Steele's Beer-Can Chicken Salad, 60
Lisa O'Brien's Beer-Poached Rosemary Chicken, 132
Oatmeal Stout-Maple-Mustard-Glazed Chicken, 134
Pale Ale Chicken Paprikash, 135
Rawleigh's Curried Beer-Can Chicken, 113
Thai Chicken Pizza with Peanut Sauce, 63
Thai Chicken Wings with Peanut Sauce, 24

crab
Crab Cakes with Beer-Reduction Remoulade, 148
Lambic Hot Crab Dip, 32
Soft-Shell Crabs in Butter and Beer, 149

Croutons, Potato Bread, 44

crusts
Basic Beer Crust for pizza, 71
Chocolate, 219
Corn Bread, 120-121
Cracker, 187
Graham Cracker, 233
Peanut Butter Graham Cracker, 242

desserts
Apple Fritters in Beer Batter with Cider Sauce, 222
Apricot Ale Cheesecake, 224
Banana Beignets with Praline Ice Cream and Rum Sauce, 226-227
BC's Orange-Ginger Cake with Bock Buttercream, 220
Chocolate Bock Beeramisu, 230
Hard Lemonade Cake, 236
Hard Lime Pie, 234
Honey-Almond Beer Cake, 232
Irish Pumpkin Pie with Guinness and Golden Raisins, 225
Lambic Pêche and Grilled Peaches and Cream, 244
Mango-Malt Mousse Pie, 233
Mocha Porter Pie, 219
Peanut Brittle Praline Beer Puffs, 240-241

Peanut Butter and Porter Pie, 242

Pineapple-Pecan Beer Bread Pudding with Brown Sugar-Beer Sauce, 245

Poached Pears in Lambic Framboise, 246

Porter-Roasted Pears with Macaroon Crumbs, 237

Raspberry-Root Beer Torte, 250

Stout and Sauerkraut Fudge Cake, 228–229

Stout Ice Cream-Praline Sundae, 248–249

Tropical Fruit Trifle, 238–239

duck

Framboise Lambic-Glazed Duckling, 117

Stout-Glazed Duck Breast, 124

eggs

Bourbon Street Brunch Eggs with Beer, 200–201

Eggs Beeradict, 188

fish

Bayou Catfish in Beer-Batter and Remoulade, 138

Beer-Baked Cod Amandine, 143

British Beer-Battered Fish and Chips, 145

Dilled Grilled Swordfish Skewers in White Ale, 150

Kirin-Glazed Salmon, 154

Pecan Crusted Trout with Porter Glaze, 137

Pilsner-Poached Salmon with Dill, 153

Stout Grilled Tuna Teriyaki Steaks with Orange Aioli, 152

Tyler's Soft Fish Tacos, 140

frosting

Bock Buttercream, 220

Chocolate-Cream Cheese, 228–229

Root Beer Cream, 250

fruit

Apple Fritters in Beer Batter with Cider Sauce, 222

Banana Beer Bread, 204

Banana Beignets with Praline Ice Cream and Rum Sauce, 226–227

Blueberry Beer Muffins, 216

Blueberry-Buckwheat Beer Pancakes, 196

Ham, Pineapple, and Porter Pizza, 76

Lambic Pêche and Grilled Peaches and Cream, 244

Mustard-Fruit Marmalade, 146

Pineapple-Pecan Beer Bread Pudding with Brown Sugar-Beer Sauce, 245

Poached Pears in Lambic Framboise, 246

Porter-Cranberry Sauce, 73

Porter-Roasted Pears with Macaroon Crumbs, 237

Tropical Fruit Trifle, 238–239

glazes

Apple and Brown Ale, 133

Chocolate, 240–241

Framboise Lambic Raspberry, 117

Oatmeal Stout-Maple-Mustard, 134

Pilsner, 96–97

Porter, 137

Rosemary Lambic Reduction, 83

Stout and Red Currant Jam, 124

hot dogs

Drunken Beer Dog Pizzas, 72

Drunken Beer Dogs, 22

Jamaican Jerk Seasoning, 131

lamb

Irish Lamb Shanks Braised in Stout, 94

Pilsner Shepherd's Pie, 98

marinades

for chicken, 116

for Rock Cornish game hens, 130–131

Teriyaki, 152

mussels

Tyler's Mussels in Guinness and Garlic, 141

pasta

Beer and Bacon Bolognese Sauce, 66

Macaroni and Beer Cheese with Bacon, 68

Penne with Porter, Pancetta, and Porcini Mushroom Sauce, 64

Pilsner Pasta and Pizza Sauce
with Sun-Dried Tomatoes, 70
Spaghetti Carbeernara, 77
pizza
Basic Beer Crust, 71
Caramelized Onion, Goat Cheese,
and Walnut, 67
Drunken Beer Dog, 72
Ham, Pineapple, and Porter, 76
Pilsner Pasta and Pizza Sauce
with Sun-Dried Tomatoes, 70
Porter-Cranberry-Pecan, 73
Portobello Mushroom, Stout, and
Swiss Flatbread, 74
Thai Chicken with Peanut Sauce,
63
pork
Apple Ale-Glazed Pork Chops,
86
Aunt BC's Pork with Porter and
Turnip Greens, 85
Backward Beerbecued Ribs with
Bourbon, 161
Pilsner-Glazed Pork Chops with
Pineapple Cilantro Salsa,
96–97
Pilsner Pulled Pork Sandwiches,
169
Porc à la Flemande, 99
Pork Ribs in Sauerkraut and
Beer, 95
Pork Stir-Fry with Bell Peppers
Porter, 102
Stout and Spicy Pork Satay,
106–107
potatoes
Beer-Battered Baked Potato
Wedges, 177
Belgian Dilled New Potatoes, 184
Danish Potato Soup with Beer,
42
German Potato Salad with
Biergarten Dressing, 56
Pale Ale au Gratin Potatoes, 181
Pilsner Mashed Potatoes with
Parsley, Chives, and Cheddar
Cheese, 182
Porter Sweet Potato Salad, 35
rice
Spinach Risotto with Pilsner and
Peas, 183

Wisconsin Beer and White
Cheddar Wild Rice Soup, 36
Rock Cornish game hens
Jamaican Jerk Grilled Rock
Cornish Game Hens, 130–131
salad dressing
Balsamic-Beer, 54
Beer-Can, 60
Beer Cheese, 58
Biergarten, 56
Cajun Vinaigrette, 51
Lambic-Lemon Vinaigrette, 55
Maple-Bacon Beer, 52
salads
Beer-Battered Cajun Popcorn
Shrimp Salad, 51
Bulgur Salad with Beer, 50
Fig Salad with Balsamic-Beer
Dressing, 54
German Potato Salad with
Biergarten Dressing, 56
Grilled Salmon Salad with
Lambic-Lemon Vinaigrette, 55
Iceberg Raft with Beer Cheese
Dressing and Bacon, 58
Lee Steele's Beer-Can Chicken
Salad, 60
Pilsner Pulled Pork Lettuce
Wraps, 59
Porter Sweet Potato Salad, 35
Spinach, Pear, and Apple Salad
with Maple-Bacon Beer
Dressing, 52
salmon
Grilled Salmon Salad with
Lambic-Lemon Vinaigrette, 55
Kirin-Glazed Salmon, 154
Pilsner-Poached Salmon with
Dill, 153
salsa
Pineapple Cilantro Salsa, 96–97
sauces
Apple Butter Beerbecue, 157
Baja, 142
Banana Rum, 226–227
Beer and Bacon Bolognese, 66
Beer and Molasses Beerbecue,
161
Beer-Reduction Remoulade, 148
Beernaise, 91

Brown Sugar-Beer, 245
Buttery Beerbecue, 160
Carolina White Beerbecue, 163
Chili-Lime Mesquite Beerbecue, 164
Chocolate Bock Syrup, 190
Cider, 222
Classic Welsh Rabbit, 198
Dill Hollandaise, 153
Guinness Praline, 248-249
Hollandaise, 200-201
Honey-Beer-Mustard, 178
Honey-Mustard Malt Vinegar Dip, 177
Irish Whiskey Beerbecue, 166
Maple Bacon Beerbecue, 167
Mustard-Fruit Marmalade, 146
Onion-Beer Gravy, 82
Orange Aioli, 152
Peanut, 24, 63, 106-107
Peppercorn Cream, 103
Pilsner Pasta and Pizza Sauce with Sun-Dried Tomatoes, 70
Porcini Mushroom, 64
Porter-Cranberry, 73
Remoulade, 138
Slow Cooker Honey Beerbecue, 167
Spicy Texas-Style Beerbecue, 171
sauerkraut
    Pork Ribs in Sauerkraut and Beer, 95
    Stout and Sauerkraut Fudge Cake, 228-229
sausage
    Beer and Sausage Strata, 192
    Slow-Cooked Knockwurst and Cabbage in Pilsner, 100
scallops
    Baja Scallops in Beer Batter, 142
shrimp
    Beer-Battered Cajun Popcorn Shrimp Salad, 51
    Beer-Broiled Shrimp, 144
    Classic Beer-Battered Shrimp with Mustard-Fruit Marmalade, 146
soups
    Asian Beer-Chicken, 38

Baby Bella Mushroom and Beer, 39
Chicken Chili with Beer and Black Beans, 40
Danish Potato with Beer, 42
Fresh Tomato and Beer, 43
Game Day Beer Cheese, 47
Oxtail, Lentil, and Lager Onion, 46
Steak and Stout Stew, 48
Stout Onion Gratin, 44
Wisconsin Beer and White Cheddar Wild Rice, 36
turkey
    Henry's Heavy-on-the-Garlic Turkey Chili with Beer, 128
    Turkey Hash Au Gratin with Porter and Potatoes, 123
    Turkey with Beer and Black-Eyed Peas, 109
veal
    Osso Buco in Beer, 80
    Veal Chops with Rosemary Lambic Reduction, 83
vegetables
    Beer-Battered Baked Potato Wedges, 177
    Beer-Battered Onion Rings, 178
    Beer-Glazed Baby Carrots, 176
    Beerbecue Baked Beans, 158
    Belgian Dilled New Potatoes, 184
    Broccoli, Blue Cheese and Beer Bake, 180
    Brussels Sprouts in Beer with Honey-Roasted Cashews, 174
    Green Bean and Portobello Mushroom Casserole with Porter, 179
    Green Beans with Portobello Mushrooms and Porter, 185
    Pale Ale au Gratin Potatoes, 181
    Pilsner Mashed Potatoes with Parsley, Chives, and Cheddar Cheese, 182
    Spinach Risotto with Pilsner and Peas, 183
    Zucchini in Beer Batter, 173

Acknowledgments

I'd like to give special thanks to Bill Boteler and Lee Steele for their editorial contribution to this book.

No book is created without a little help from your friends. I also want to thank the following people for their recipes, taste testing and support during this project: Paul Arroyo, Lisa O'Brien, James Comstock, BC Molinare, Rawleigh Morse, Henry Schaffer, and Tyler and David Taylor.

About the Author

Alison Boteler is a newspaper columnist and magazine contributor whose credits include the *Connecticut Post*, *Fairfield County Weekly*, and *Family Fun* magazine. Her career began at an early age with cooking spots for kids on WNEW's *Wonderama* and regular appearances on *Midday Live with Bill Boggs* in New York City. While in college, she hosted her own radio show, *Alison's Restaurant*, on WCWP FM and had Julia Child as one of her first guests. After graduation, she made appearances on NBC's *Today Show* and later became a regular on Lifetime's *Our Home*. She has been a creative consultant to several major food companies and is the author of *The Gourmet's Guide to Cooking with Wine*, Quarry Books, 2008. This is her tenth book. Alison lives in Connecticut.